Nick & Ma

THE

~~ABC~~

X Y Z

OF

Discipleship

Understanding and Reaching
Generations Y&Z

malcolm down
PUBLISHING

23 22 21 20 19   7 6 5 4 3 2 1

First published 2020 by
Malcolm Down Publishing Ltd.
www.malcolmdown.co.uk

British Library Cataloguing in Publication Data
A catalogue record for this book is available from the British Library.

ISBN 978-1-912863-43-3

Front cover design by Stephen Bradley Instagram: mrstephenbradley
Additional design by Esther Kotecha
Art direction by Sarah Grace

Printed in the UK

Nick and Marjorie are the real deal. XYZ is not only the fruit of years of faithful investment and learning from living and breathing young adult culture, it is a much-needed manifesto to inspire hope and prophetically call the Church to both adapt to the winds of cultural change and hold steadfastly to the gospel and radical kingdom living. This book is a must for every church leader. May we, as a Church, receive its wisdom, apply it to our contexts and see many twenties and thirties come to faith in Jesus.

Phil Knox, Head of Mission to Young Adults, Evangelical Alliance UK, and author

In knowing Nick and Marjorie for over a decade, their passion for introducing the lost and unchurched to Jesus has never wavered. They are the real deal and live their lives away from the pulpit following everything they preach. Their lives and family are open, and 'doing life' with people is kingdom-focused and Spirit-led.

In this book *The XYZ of Discipleship* they challenge us to look beyond our church programmes in order to create intentional environments and connection for discipleship with the Generations Y and Z. They address how to how redefine discipleship for them by capturing their hearts and value systems. All without diluting the glorious truth of the gospel of Jesus Christ and the Word of God. They are not afraid of the perceived threat of challenge by Generations Y and Z but see it as a foundation to lead them to love and devotion to Jesus and His plans in their lives and callings.

This book is a must read for anyone leading a church today!

Duncan and Kate Smith, Presidents, Catch the Fire World and Senior Leaders Catch the Fire Church Raleigh-Durham, North Carolina and authors

I have absolutely LOVED reading this book. It is such a wise and valuable contribution to the vital task of discipling contemporary young adults. A profound survey of the landscape of contemporary culture combined with a comprehensive overview of discipleship which is authentically biblical, and laced with practical wisdom born out of years of pastoral experience and cultural understanding. This is a vital resource for all those who long to make sense of the challenges and complexities of today's world and to enable its natives to thrive as Christian disciples. It deserves to be widely read.

Rev Ian Parkinson, CPAS leadership development specialist; Associate Lecturer St Mellitus College; Associate Lecturer St Hild College, and author

In this book, Nick and Marjorie open a door into young adult ministry that few others can. They do a crucial job of clearing out half-formed stereotypes, confronting the Church's fear of failure and clarifying the key issues. Moments into reading it I was filled with new passion, new ideas and new hope for the emerging generations.

What sets this book apart is the way it has been honed in real life and real ministry: the mistakes, the vulnerability and the many gems of kingdom wisdom that result. There are ideas here for every kind of church to try, set out in a passionate manual that's also generous and easy to engage with. And uniting the whole volume is a theology which is biblically inspired, culturally aware and open to the wide, wild work of the Spirit.

Through these pages, young adults call out to the Church for a faith that is humanly real and spiritually empowered – God, give us the courage to answer the call!

Rev Canon Mark Powley, Principal, St Hild College, and author.

For anyone seeking to evangelise and disciple Generations Y and Z, Nick and Marjorie's book offers a wealth of insight from their experiences and life-wisdom of working among this generation. As they point out, there is great spiritual hunger and need among this age group, but in an environment where the Church is struggling to reach this demographic, their book is a much-needed resource.

Dr Lucy Peppiatt, Principal, Westminster Theological Centre, and author

Nick and Marjorie certainly live what they teach in *The XYZ of Discipleship*. They have the rare credibility that comes from real-life experience loving, leading and learning from the very generations they are teaching about here. The book has a lot of depth, and many genuine insights into an area of ministry that, let's face it, hasn't been a strong point for the Church in recent times. In a time of much confusion, and in places, increasing desperation as we watch Generations Y and Z walk away from Church community, the Allans offer genuine clarity, and an approach that is pastoral and helpful. I especially appreciate their sensitivity in dealing with many difficult topics, and their focus on celebrating and learning from the varied strengths of people from these age groups. I honestly believe this book presents the Church with an essential guide for including, discipling and empowering such brilliantly creative and communal people, and I hope that we will all learn from it as we seek to do this well. Thank you, Nick and Marjorie, for providing something so timely and valuable, borne out of your many years of ministry and learning in these areas.

Dr Daniel McGinnis, Church Planter, Executive Director Leeds School of Theology, Vice Principal St Hild College, and author

If I wanted to build a house, I would hire someone who is skilled in building houses that stand the test of time. It would be important for me to know that my builder has some experience in creating homes that people want to live in to create a family. I would have very little desire to sit down and discuss my house plans with someone who had great ideas, but no experience in actually building homes. When I found out that my friends Nick and Marjorie Allan were writing a book on reaching Generations Y and Z, I knew I would enjoy it because I know who they are as spouses, parents and pastors. They have a lot of experience in actually doing what they write about in *The XYZ of Discipleship*. This book is not written from a place of philosophy, rather it is written from a place of experience in reaching these two targets. As you read this book, you will enjoy an honest and straightforward account of the challenges we face as pastors and leaders. After reading this book, I believe you will have some new strategies on successfully navigating some new terrain as we help these generations connect deeply to God and each other.

Chad Norris, Senior Pastor Bridgeway Church, Greenville SC, author, host of *Coach & Joe* Podcast.

Nothing will change in our efforts to reach the 'missing generation' if they remain the 'misunderstood generation' . . . so we're grateful to Nick and Marjorie for sharing what they've learned about engaging, reaching and releasing this amazing generation into kingdom service!

Rev Paul Harcourt, National Leader, New Wine England, and author

Nick and Marjorie have been friends for many years and throughout that time have demonstrated a significant gift for attracting young adults, seeing them, bringing security into their lives and raising them up to be champions.

They have never been restricted by culture or by trends but have had a supernatural flexibility to reach everyone they meet and empower everyone they meet. This book will open a door for you to do the same to those God has given to you.

Stuart & Chlo Glassborow, Senior Leaders Catch the Fire World and church planters of CTF London, Founders of The Kenyan Children's Project NGO

We all know the UK and wider Western Church needs to face up to the challenge of reaching today's young adults and young people, but where should we start?

Of course, we should pray for help from our God who knows all of us better than we know ourselves, including those in the Millennial generation and younger. Secondly, we need to hear from key church leaders who have experience of fruitful ministry working alongside those who fall within Generation Y and Generation Z and this is where this helpful new book from Marjorie and Nick Allan fills a needed gap.

What strikes me most in reading *The XYZ of Discipleship* is a refreshing optimism and confidence for us all seeing more fruitful discipleship among these key age groups.

Marjorie and Nick helpfully explain how some of the negativity directed towards generations Y and Z is often unfair and comes from misunderstandings. They argue that there are new and specific kingdom opportunities among young and emerging adults because so many of them are spiritually open and have often seen, in their parents' generations, the inadequacy of being spiritually closed.

Marjorie and Nick have drawn on experience from others wherever necessary, but it is their own story at The Well and their own personal experiences of key people in their lives when they were young adults which gives particular credibility to their words.

They have carved out time for these missing generations in their church by keeping 'first things first' and being prepared to say the needed, brave 'no's to the many things which can occupy too much of a church leader's time. Once they have made that time, they have given it away freely, spending hours, rather than minutes, in their home and church with young people, seeking to understand, mentor and empower them. They believe in releasing the next generation to dream and 'have a good go', alongside creating contexts for powerful encounters of the presence of God.

As well as being a book for generations Y and Z, this book reminds me, as a parent with adult children of my own in the generation Z category, of the areas where I too am a product of this age. Aspects of the culture of these generations have spilled over to all of us. Some of the insights in this book are therefore not just limited to certain ages but to the age in which we all find ourselves.

Rev Ken Benjamin, President of Baptists Together 2019-20, Director of Church Relationships, The London Institute for Contemporary Christianity (LICC)

Acknowledgements

We love being part of the Baptist family in the UK, who are flexible and pragmatic, missional-minded and led by the Scriptures and the Spirit. We are very grateful to the Baptists Together team at Didcot who agreed to fund our research and production of this book. We hope it helps to inspire and inform the whole movement.

Many thanks to our friends and family of The Well Sheffield, and our fantastic staff and volunteer team. In many ways, this is your story and we love the journey we are all on together.

We are so grateful for the Christian input and example we've received over the years from a few significant leaders. Willi and Ruth, Mike and Sally, Mal and Chriscelle, Paul and Elly, Lucy and Nick, you gave of yourselves and you modelled your own discipleship journeys to us, challenging and inspiring us to grow to be more like Jesus. Likewise, our own parents have been beautiful examples to us, loving Christians who are focused on discipleship and generous, missionary lives.

Thanks to our close community of people we've journeyed with in Sheffield for many years. Some of you are really 'extended family' to us and have supported us through thick and thin, helping us to preach what we practise and to practise what we preach. We love you.

Thank you to Malcolm, our publisher, Sheila, our editor, Stephen and Ben, our design and online gurus.

Finally, thank you to our three wonderful children for all your patience during the year it took to write and edit this work. You are our first discipleship focus, and we are so very proud of your lives and characters.

Contents

Section Four: Our Response

Foreword

I have the huge privilege of offering spiritual leadership to a movement of UK churches called Baptists Together. What I have come to realise is that one of our biggest kingdom assets are our many incredible, Christ-centred, passionate, missional and creative leaders. Nick and Marjorie Allan definitely count in that number. It was my colleague, Graham Ensor, who first introduced me to Nick and Marjorie, and right from the start I have been inspired by their heart for the Lord and their bold vision to plant churches and connect with students and young adults. They are a couple with a wealth of spiritual wisdom and experience who are seasoned church planters, compassionate disciplers, reflective practitioners, gifted prophets and urban missionaries. But this is not simply something they do; it is who they are. They walk the talk in their own following of Jesus and encourage many others on that journey too. While we are blessed that Nick and Marjorie would count Baptists as their 'home base', I know that they are also held in very high regard in different Church streams both here in the UK and globally, and rightly so.

When Marjorie first pitched the idea of this book to me, in a car park on an industrial estate in Stafford, I was in! I could immediately see the timely and fruitful combination of a book about discipling young adults coming from a couple who have a proven track record of ministry in this area. And, at a time when so many churches are increasingly aware of the need to encourage and reach these generations, an insightful, practical and accessible book like this will be invaluable to inspire and give confidence to anyone who reads it.

The first thing that reading this book will offer you is a perceptive insight into the world view of Generations Y and Z. Moving beyond the sound bites and stereotypes, Nick and Marjorie will help you to climb into the experiences, assumptions, attitudes, hopes and fears of these generations and what they care about; illustrated not just in what they write but also through the stories and case studies that they share. Having done this, the authors then take the reader on a further journey to enable us to see not only the distinctives of young adults, but more importantly the preciousness of these generations and how they positively enrich churches and communities in so many ways. If you started this book looking for ways to mitigate against the negative stereotypes of the 'snowflake generation' in your church, then I am sure that you will end the book eager to serve alongside such passionate 'all-in' disciples!

But don't make the mistake of thinking that this book is merely a glossy PR job for students and young adults. As you get into the book you will see how Nick and Marjorie also offer a thoughtful and theological critique that seeks to identify and challenge some of the underlying cultural assumptions of these generations and explore what the nature of God and the lordship of Christ means for those who are seeking to follow Jesus and become more like him.

Being a practical church leader myself, I love where the book ends up as Nick and Marjorie unpack the implications of connecting with students and young adults for churches. Please make sure that you don't miss this vital section! And what I believe is really profound here is that what Marjorie and Nick advocate is not just good for young adults; it is the sort of church we all want to be part of. So, let's bring it on! A Christ-centred, Spirit-filled community where we dream kingdom dreams together and we create a permission-giving culture where it is safe to take risks and you know that people are cheering you on; where we nurture loving, authentic and vulnerable communities and where our patterns of leadership and being church are rooted in genuine relationship, shared discipleship and common mission rather than institutional structures of bygone eras.

Finally, I hope that in reading this book you will, like me, not just find out more *about* young adults and leave it at that. I hope that you will take up the challenge that Nick and Marjorie offer as they close. If you are over thirty-five, never forget that these generations have grown up in a culture that has been shaped and nurtured by us. So, we need to be part of the change we are longing for, and making sure that our discipleship is rooted in Christ more than in our prevailing culture. This has got to start with me and you, but I pray that it will become a journey where all the generations will spur one another on in seeking God's kingdom first, because that will be a beautiful thing. I want to be part of that, and I hope that you do too.

Lynn Green
General Secretary, Baptists Together in Great Britain
February 2020

Introduction

I will teach you hidden lessons from our past – stories we have heard and known, stories our ancestors handed down to us.

We will not hide these truths from our children; we will tell the next generation about the glorious deeds of the LORD, about his power and his mighty wonders.

. . . So each generation should set its hope anew on God, not forgetting his glorious miracles and obeying his commands.

(Psalm 78:2-4,7)

This book is about discipleship, discipleship to Jesus. Specifically, it is about how to disciple young adults and those approaching their twenties, and how to do that in the middle of today's British and Western culture. Generation Y (born between c.1981-96) and Generation Z (c.1996-2014) are sometimes called the 'missing generation' from the UK Church, yet they are thriving and expanding their influence within the rest of society. Can we bridge the gap? Can we understand the cultural landscape they inhabit and work out how best to reach them with the gospel, helping them to become followers of Jesus?

You may be an older individual or a church leader who knows instinctively that something has to change 'on our watch'. You may be of Generations Y or Z yourself, desperate to follow Jesus wholeheartedly and to help others to do the same. This work is not another attempt to box people or make sweeping generalisations. It is written from our own desire to understand these generations who are being shaped and discipled all the time by contemporary culture. Individuals and the Church today have the opportunity and responsibility to help the young to be shaped instead as disciples of Jesus, with their identity and purpose founded upon the narrative of the Bible, and to navigate contemporary culture better as a result.

Over the past twenty-five years since we, the authors, were in our early twenties, we have asked ourselves these kind of questions and spent countless hours around the discipleship of young adults as we have led churches full of them. In the UK today there are numbers of churches and people seeing fruit in this area, and we applaud them all. This work is our attempt to bring together good practice both in what discipleship can look like for individuals, and how our local churches can shape an effective response in these challenging times.

What is discipleship? Nick and Marjorie's stories

Fan to follower to friend to family (Marjorie's story)

I became a follower of Jesus standing in the front square of Trinity College Dublin one cold autumn night during my university Freshers' week. I had just attended a debate between the Philosophical Society and the Christian Union entitled: 'Did Jesus Christ live, die and rise from the dead?' Both sides had chosen brilliant orators and the atmosphere in the old atrium was electric. In retrospect, I recognise that the presence of God descended in that room and I had a revelation of the truth. That night, looking up at the stars, I remember thinking 'If that is true, I will become your follower.' What I decided then, I hold to this day.

I did know about Jesus previously. You might have described me as a fan. I believed He was real and I knew something of how attractive and indeed how powerful He was since I had been instantly and dramatically physically healed as a teenager when some Christians laid hands on me and prayed. It took longer for me to become a follower – that was when I recognised that accepting the truth about Jesus comes on His terms, not mine. He calls us to lay down our lives, to follow in His footsteps. I am forever indebted to the group of college students who modelled to me at that time a relationship with Jesus. They carried Bibles around and read them. They got up early to pray. They were very keen to share their faith with their friends on campus.

As I have journeyed as a disciple, I have increasingly found that discipleship to Jesus best flows from friendship with Him. 'I no longer call you slaves . . . Now you are my friends' (John 15:15). During my mid-twenties I lived and ministered among radical Youth With A Mission (YWAM) teams who taught and demonstrated friendship with our Father God. Slowly that became my reality too. There is a further level of revelation, that of being family with God. Into my thirties, Nick and I were helped by mentors around us to comprehend our truest spiritual identity as a much-loved daughter and son of God. I began to operate from a deep level of security and felt free to step out knowing that because I am a child of God, I now have nothing to prove and nothing to lose. This is the kind of life I want to model and pass on to others today.

Facedown in a field (Nick's story)

I made a decision to follow Jesus — really follow him and surrender to His ways and His call on my life — when I was about twenty-three. Growing up in a Christian home as a 'Preacher's Kid' I thought I knew plenty *about* God. I was influential in church and I had surrendered my life aged seventeen. But a change needed to come. It took me a long time to realise for myself that I wasn't really following Him. I wasn't sold out, I wasn't yet willing to carry my cross, I wasn't fully apprenticed to His ways. In short, and in common with so many young adults in every era, I had a lot more surrendering to do. Finally, at a Christian summer camp I made a decision, prompted I am sure by the Holy Spirit within me. If God was as real as I believed, then He was worth me surrendering *everything* to follow His ways above mine. I knelt down alone in a grassy field and I spoke out my wholehearted 'yes' and 'do it your way' and on that day I truly began to become a disciple of Jesus.

Many, many more times I would find myself on my face before God. My church in those days was brimming with young adults on a similar journey. At every Sunday service we would be encouraged to respond to the message or to whatever the Holy Spirit was saying and doing with us by kneeling or lying down in prayer and genuine submission, knowing that in God's grace we would get up empowered and ready to change. Repentance and faith are key processes of discipleship, as Jesus says in Mark 1:15. In my twenties, during those formative years as I began a career in marketing and later married, many people helped me to shape my life and my priorities around God. They gave me patience and time, food and friendship. They shared their homes and families with me, they challenged me and put me into uncomfortable and stretching situations. They showed me what it means to live as a disciple, and as a result they taught me how to raise others as disciples too. I am eternally grateful.

The UK at a crossroads

Arguably the UK today is at its most significant time of change since the Second World War; we live in pivotal times. The cultural landscape is shifting at a sometimes-bewildering pace. There are huge changes affecting all generations and in particular the young. We are witnessing a curious paradox. The breakdown of our political norms and landscapes but a democratisation through social media. Distrust in institutions and in leadership but a search for authenticity. An undercurrent of fear and terror but a rise of activism, and the turmoil of a fragile economy but the growth of artisans and entrepreneurialism. Values are morphing fast as the technological revolution plays out its global implications. Yet amid these challenges, a powerful young generation is rising whose voice and passion for causes like the environment are inspiring others into action. The future belongs to them, but how will the Christians react in the present?

Christianity is no longer the dominant world view in Britain; it no longer provides the framework for society in terms of morality, family, aspirations or beliefs. The Christian Church is a muted subculture considered by many to be out of touch, intolerant, or just one of many lifestyle choices today. Britain has experienced a massive shift in identity, so that spirituality or ways of belonging are no longer expressed through the traditional pillars of politics, localism or religion. The Christian remnant, otherwise known as the Church, is floundering to construct a coherent response which calls people towards our passion and commitment to Christ. It is a similar picture in most western nations, and even the United States is arguably now travelling in that direction.

But there are glimmers of hope, because the Spirit of God never gives up on our nations and humanity. Generations Y and Z are some of the most spiritually hungry this nation has known in decades. And humanity hasn't changed all that much. Young adults in every era will question reality, search their souls and search the universe for depth of meaning. Human beings are always spiritual beings. This is where hope lies for those young people rising today. As the Church grows in understanding Generations Y and Z we will get better at reaching them, and in discipling those who choose to follow Christ.

Not going to be easy

Nobody says this is going to be easy! This book has four sections of analysis and recommendations:

1. Starting with the positive potential of Generations Y and Z, we outline some common traits in the way they view the world, how they act or express themselves, and we bring challenge to some of our society's more negative assumptions. We see

a tremendous opportunity for Christ-like discipleship and outline how mature Christians can mentor young adults to this end.

2. Our identity in Christ is the foundation of fruitful discipleship. In a battlefield of individualism we look carefully at the benefits of community and vulnerability, painting a picture of how best a young adult can view themselves in the light of Christ.

3. There a number of specific issues which can be unhelpful strongholds in young adult culture. We address the challenges of relativism, Fear Of Missing Out, and how to be generously inclusive.

4. How can the UK and Western Church respond? We outline some strengths to play to and some changes to be made so that local churches may get better at reaching and raising young adult disciples.

Some definitions

'Generation Y' are the cohort often known as the Millennials, since they reached young adulthood in the early twenty-first century, being born between approximately 1981 to 1996. This is no longer a new generation, they represent about 14 per cent of the total UK population (32 per cent worldwide)[1] and are integrated into places of work and education. They have been studied and feted by the advertising industry; they are beginning now to hold some of the most responsible positions in society.

'Generation Z' may be variously known as Plurals, iGeneration or Centennials. They were born from around 1996 to 2014, meaning some of them are still in primary school as we write, while others have recently graduated university. This is the generation entering today's workforce.

Generation X were born roughly from around 1965 to 1980. They are in many of the positions of authority and responsibility in their working and family lives, and are the parents of the majority of Generation Z.

'Young Adults' or 'Emerging Adults' is a broad and perhaps an unusual term. It describes the journey and process that young people go through in their twenties and into their thirties of growing and maturing. Our writing focuses upon the present twenties to thirties Generation Y, and on the higher end of the most recent Generation Z, the eldest of whom are about twenty-three years old (in 2020).

And a disclaimer . . .

We acknowledge upfront that there will be some generalities and perhaps even stereotypes reflected in what is written. Nevertheless, we have endeavoured to be as specific as possible about the process of discipleship and the idiosyncrasies of the generations. We do not always make the distinction between Generation Y or Z in our examples, because Gen Z is yet to be fully formed in its identity and characteristics. It is important to us that Millennials themselves have inputted into the creation of this book and some chapters have case studies written by young adults we know. But let's be honest, there is no single 'one size fits all' description or experience of young adulthood. It is impossible to be nuanced in every observation of two generations and of contemporary culture in the West. Please take the gist of what we are saying and try to not to be offended.

About the authors

As the saying goes, 'Write about what you know.' We (Nick and Marjorie) are in our mid-forties and have been leading within church for the past twenty-five years. All of that time we have learned and led among young adults in a variety of contexts including poor inner-city, suburban family church and overseas. By age thirty, we had married and settled in Sheffield, a post-industrial city in the heart of England. The decade following saw us leading three different churches: a passionate former house church which grew to replace its own 'missing generation' of twenty-somethings; then St Thomas' Philadelphia, a large Anglican/Baptist church pioneering missional communities where around 50 per cent of the church were under the age of forty, during which time Nick was ordained as a Baptist minister. Together with our congregations we took some radical journeys with God and experienced 'signs and wonders' (see Rom. 15:19), seeing large numbers of people come to faith and baptised.

In 2015 together with a small team of friends we began a church plant in the centre of the city called The Well Sheffield (www.wellsheffield.com). It is located in a popular student and young professional area. We are a missional people focused on the unchurched and de-churched because from day one we have emphasised training in how to share our faith and to disciple others. It has grown rapidly, particularly among young adults/students/young families and today we enjoy the full range of ages and messiness of a church reaching the lost. Every week there are stories of people turning to God. As the book progresses we share parts of this exciting story and something of the journey towards transformation and discipleship in people's lives.

---

1. *'Briefing Paper Number CBP7946, 11 April 2017 Millennials,'* (London: House of Commons Library, 2017) http://researchbriefings.files.parliament.uk/documents/CBP-7946/CBP-7946.pdf (accessed 11.03.2020)

SECTION ONE

Obstacles or Opportunities?

Millennials have come in for some stick for pulling society up for outdated attitudes, but defining them by what they want to curb risks missing what they want to create.

Lucy Purdy, *Positive.News*[2]

CHAPTER ONE

Misunderstood Millennials

Have you labelled me?

At a glance, the current generation of young adults appear to be more criticised than any before. Dubbed as overentitled 'snowflakes', they certainly pick up some bad press, which must feel hugely frustrating to those among them who live very differently from this, or to those who may feel their core values and lifestyle choices are being misunderstood. An examination of their core beliefs and why they may be misunderstood by older generations is hugely important if the different generations are to work well together in any church setting, and indeed in the home and workplace, and to draw out the best in each other.

It is a big mistake to label and examine any generation in isolation. We are all shaped by each other. If we deride this generation for expecting trophies simply for showing up, then we must acknowledge that somebody bought and presented those trophies to them.

In church life the danger is that a culture of misunderstood Millennials is allowed to develop, whereby older generations live with a sense of superiority and judgement upon the younger generation who, frustrated by this, are likely to remove themselves from church altogether.

This would be a catastrophic mistake.

Through no fault of their own, this emerging generation is perhaps more emotionally broken than previous ones, or at least they are more aware of their frailties. In other ways, they are remarkably resilient and admirable. They desperately need and long for the love, empowerment, guidance and wisdom of those who have lived life a little longer.

In addition, the Church as a whole is impoverished without them. These are the generations who will come up with creative solutions to problems, passionately commit to a cause and apply a new level of creativity to the whole of church life and its cause. The Church is a lot richer when these generations are actively engaged on the streets, on the stages and around strategy tables.

What lens are you looking through?

At the root of many of our frustrations and misunderstandings lies an inability to understand the core beliefs of this generation: in other words, what they value most. Sometimes these appear rather paradoxical, with conflicting realities. For example, we are told that Western culture is now more individualistic and ego-centric than ever before, most aptly portrayed by our obsession with the 'selfie'. Yet this is also the generation that would rather operate in collaborative teams in the workplace and gives very high regard to peer reviews. Today's self-employed young entrepreneurs team up around shared workstations in far less individualistic working environments than those of their predecessors. This is the emerging generation that has found a sense of family in places such as fitness studios. We have moved past the sterile gym floor of a decade ago, when strangers would exercise side by side in their individual bubbles. Instead, the young are packing out group classes and 'Boot Camps' to exercise collectively.

So which is true? Are they individualistic or community-driven?

Hobart and Sendek in their book *Gen Y Now*, identify from their research seven consistent stereotypes/myths associated with young adults:[3]

1. Lazy/slacker
2. Instant gratification, trophies for showing up
3. Narcissistic
4. Disloyal
5. Spoilt and pampered
6. Lack of respect for hierarchy and authority
7. Entitled

However, the reality may be very different. People's lives are very complex. We have heard business owners express their concern and frustration at how employed young adults sometimes come across as fragile, clock-watching and jobs-worth. To them, time in the office clearly equals commitment and quality. But Generation Y have been raised in a culture where people work on-the-go and save time by doing their emails while waiting in the coffee queue. In their minds, tasks can be picked up from anywhere, anytime. They may leave the office simply because they can – this is a flexible and fluid generation. In terms of productivity and personal well-being, both employees and employers may actually be much better served this way. It just depends which lens you are looking through.

Putting down prejudices

As the years pass, perhaps one of the greatest temptations is to see one's experiences and personal judgements, which can seem so very different in comparison with the younger generations, as superior. As disciple-makers we are never to raise followers who look like us, but rather Christ. We want them to 'imitate me . . . as I imitate Christ' (1 Cor. 11:1); recognising that the Christ-like nature developed in those around me may find its expression very differently than it did within me and my generation.

For example, Marjorie was raised as a middle-class Gen X with a strong sense of choosing and developing a career. Her parents of the 'builder generation' were raised expecting not to make significant changes along their career paths and to stay in the same company for years, or even life. None of Marjorie's peers have done this, but once they had finished training or university they still made choices to work their way up a career ladder. We are frequently reminded that the young people around us today view things very differently. The Millennial generation, now in many significant positions of leadership across this nation, work far fewer hours generally than their predecessors in their quest for a better work/life and 'whole life' balance. More important than any career is the 'purpose' of their work. It is very important to them that the purpose of the organisation they are working for matches their own value set. Hence, they will frequently swap jobs after a relatively short period of time. What to some might appear like career suicide, lack of commitment and potentially a lack of integrity could arguably have the effect of shaping a more radical disciple of Jesus since through this fluidity a person gains broader life experience, maturity, authenticity and commitment to a cause.

It just depends on the lens.

We have to tread carefully. Discipleship is all about Jesus (not us!). Mentoring is all about listening, understanding and seeing through another person's lens. There are no perfect people and every generation has its blind spots. That is why the Christian Church operates best where the generations intermix, learn from and empower each other.

When we were new leaders of a local church we particularly remember struggling with the attitude and behaviour of one young man in his early twenties. It seemed to us that he walked with an attitude and air of entitlement, assuming that he could change the world single-handed. We would regularly chat about how we would address and challenge this. We tried being firm, blunt and uncompromising. We tried to come alongside him and encourage him into more healthy attitudes. Frankly, we did not quite know what to do. While some of this was simply the natural behaviour of an immature post-adolescent, it took us some years to realise that this young man was not trying to be difficult or different, he simply reflected his generation. He was a Millennial through and through. It surprised us to begin with but over time we have come to see so many common traits in others of his era. He is now in his early thirties and still a very typical Millennial. Today we would approach discipling such a young man differently rather than just assume we needed somehow to beat these attitudes out of him.

It is not possible to confront existing prejudices in a church or people-group until you take an honest look and confront them in yourself. It is imperative to lay these down along with our perhaps legitimate frustrations if we are to play our part in shaping the leaders and disciples of the future. Today's generations have been given many different labels. Some are positive, like being the 'solutions generation', others are negative, like being 'touchy, homeless, and helpless'. We write-off these emerging adults at our peril. It is time for the Church to smash the stereotypes and embrace these generations who have fire in their bellies.

---

3. Buddy Hobart and Herb Sendek, *Gen Y Now: Millennials and the Evolution of Leadership* (San Francisco, CA: Wiley, 2nd edition, 2014).

CHAPTER TWO

Concentrate on Culture

The right kind of culture

Our emerging generations see life through a different lens, and those of us seeking to disciple them need to be willing to allow for our own perceptions, expectations and even prejudices to be challenged and amended in response. The contemporary Church must wake up and be asking the right questions of ourselves and our discipleship culture.

Culture may broadly be defined as a people-group's values, beliefs, behaviours, language and symbols, intellectual achievements, artistic expression and their lifestyle. As culture shifts and develops around us we have to be flexible in our response to it. Nevertheless, 2,000 years of Christian history has also taught us that some principles and practices of training our minds and bodies in obedience to Christ never change (2 Cor. 10:5; 1 Tim. 4:7).

A decade ago, when we were leading in a large young adult church, one of our challenges was discipleship in the midst of a celebrity culture. It sometimes felt like a pick 'n' mix sweet shop as young people chose to be influenced by any number of individuals or popular megachurches across a burgeoning online world. As their local leaders we might say, 'It's great that you listen to a famous church in California for your main teachings, but it's also important to listen to local leaders too. The Californian culture is a bit different to Sheffield!' Or, 'It's wonderful that you are inspired to be like missionaries out in Africa. So what does that mean for you as a student in Sheffield? What does the missional kind of life look like in the present?'

Today's conversation is slightly different. 'We don't do celebrity Christianity, so we won't be coming to hear this visiting speaker,' they tell us. 'We would rather have the authentic leader whose life we can see.' This thinking works well if they have good local leaders inspiring and shaping their lives, but many young people across our churches are probably being shaped the most by secular online social media. The carefully crafted presentation of vloggers and podcasters appeals to people craving entertainment or real-life drama, but their content is usually a million miles away from a discipleship narrative. If the average Christian young person in the UK only makes it to church or their small group perhaps only once in the month, it is clear who is and who is not primarily shaping them. They miss out on the value of deep community, of engaging with helpful discipleship rhythms and receiving God's graces from leaders and adults more experienced and overflowing in the power of the Holy Spirit.

Concentrate on culture not vision

So how could the Church and its leaders respond to such challenges? Let us start positively with the reality that if the challenges are huge and the pitfalls are many, then so too are the opportunities. 'O Israel, hope in the LORD; for with the LORD there is unfailing love. His redemption overflows' (Ps. 130:7).

We have been leading churches now for the past fifteen years, and young adults for the past twenty-five years. Over that time, we have come to appreciate that it is the culture of a church, rather than its vision, which achieves lasting discipleship and church growth. We have worked in contexts where great emphasis is placed upon vision and strong vision statements were articulated in detail. However, God often tweaks or changes a church's vision! We follow God's mission, not the other way around, and He unfolds things that we could never have anticipated or planned for.

It is a healthy culture that achieves the vision of an organisation. A culture focused upon seeking and training towards God's kingdom will produce consistent results whatever amendments may come to a church's vision. Culture is the kind of people you want to be, what you hold as values to shape you and others. Culture is how an organisation 'feels' to somebody and it demonstrates what we value in action. As the well-known business maxim goes: 'Culture eats strategy for breakfast.'

Understanding their culture

There are brilliant examples across the business world of individuals who understood the importance of culture. One of our favourites is Richard Branson and his books such as *Losing My Virginity* and *The Virgin Way*. He lets us into his heart and head as to how he dreamt up the Virgin culture with its emphasis upon building fun and community in positive, relaxed, and bright environments. He has consistently rolled out this culture whatever the context and whatever the era, from trains and planes to banks and gyms. You will always find the same environment and feel, the bright red and white colours and the same happy, smiley staff.

We can really learn from this type of success as churches. Are our environments actually attractive? Would people want to be there? If our expectation is for multiplication of people and people's lives, only a consistent culture will allow us to be confident in what is actually being multiplied. Does our culture actually lend itself to raising and empowering young, radical followers of Jesus? Is there opportunity for them to be mentored by older, wiser heads? Is ours a genuinely empowering culture that raises multiple young people to express themselves, or is it centred around one or two strong characters? Is there an opportunity for young adults to lead on the stage? Is there an opportunity for them to dream and start something new, perhaps a kingdom venture beyond the church walls or in the marketplace? Is it a place where it is safe for people to be challenged to become more Christ-like because relationships are strong?

Case Study:

Dr Tim Keller and Redeemer Presbyterian Church in New York City

While we do not all need to become social and cultural commentators to have role in discipling the younger generations, any wise cross-cultural missionary will spend hours of their time observing the culture they are trying to reach. When Dr Tim Keller, a well-known church leader in New York City, was asked to plant a new church into Manhattan in 1989, he and his team initially spent months firstly understanding the city, and subsequent months understanding the people-group they were intending to reach. Research showed them that the unreached people-groups of New York City at the time were the young professionals, the artists and the gay community. Keller then gave hours to meeting these local people in an effort to understand their desires, hopes and fears in life. He then thought carefully about how to present the 'good news' to this group: what language, symbols, communication to use and so forth. As they planted the new church, their services were designed to honour and express their Christian values but to be accessible to the unchurched. Today the Sunday church attendance is approximately more than 5,000 and they continue to engage with, and have earned the right to speak into, a surrounding culture that they have taken care to understand.

Creating culture: Seeds on a Petrie dish

The English word 'culture' is derived from the latin *colere* meaning 'to till, cultivate'. It refers to the nurturing and care of land or animals. Another original meaning is 'honour'.[4] Culture is what we create, and what we give honour to.

It is very important that we commit to understanding the current culture young people are developing and simply find themselves within if we are to understand and invest in them. Culture is a complex thing. Sociologists differ on how it is formed. Some say it is imposed from the generation above. This would suggest, for example, that Millennials act with entitlement because they were raised by their 'Boomer' or Generation X parachute parents for whom little Billy's happiness must be achieved at all costs. Others would say that it is defined bottom-up in a response to the practices of their parents and predecessors. For example, young adults today often express their desire for committed family relationships because they have lived through many broken marriages of their parents and parents' friends. Culture also reacts to significant external factors such as 9/11 terrorism or an economic recession.

Sometimes leaders express to us that they don't know where to begin in terms of dreaming or creating a discipleship culture within their church/context, and nor do they simply want to copy a set of values from a book. We have learned to keep things very simple. To model our church and culture on the early Church in the book of Acts. Just as in horticulture or science to take some small seeds, nurture them and watch them grow. Seeds on a Petri dish in a laboratory need careful attention, warmth, moisture etc. for growth, but given the right conditions, they may grow exponentially.

Heaven's culture on earth

At The Well Sheffield we guard the culture and values of our church very carefully but we hold our vision statement very broadly. Vision changes. We planted with the stated intention of reaching the city for Jesus. We are still serving our city but from day one God also said 'and the nations' and we have grown to look like a base to send and receive overseas missionaries as well as a local church. God had a plan that was bigger and different to what we first imagined. It is better when He sets the church's vision statements and we partner with Him by creating the kind of culture in which the seeds of discipleship and mission may grow.

Cultural formation is complex, but committed Christians have a key role to play and unique perspectives, passion and power to bring. We are ambassadors of a kingdom of God culture which spans all generations. We are citizens of another world. With the right attention we may create a rich soil in which people can dream and shape their lives and society around establishing a heavenly culture 'on earth, as it is in heaven' (Matt. 6:10).

As a starter, a good question to ask is what does the culture of your church/home/organisation feel like for somebody of Generation Y and Z? Do they align with your values? Do they see and share the purpose and feel they have a part to play? Do they feel that people are trying to value, understand and accommodate them even if there is a way to go? And how do your congregation or people feel about the young generations?

---

4. 'colere', Latdict, latin-dictionary.net/search/latin/colere (accessed 03.02.20).

CHAPTER THREE

It's Got to be Meaningful: Discipleship According to Jesus

I am learning from Jesus to live my life as He would live my life if He were me.

(Dallas Willard)[5]

Understand what I believe in. It will help you to empower and challenge me

When we planted The Well Sheffield we aimed to create a culture of momentum where people could dream and start new initiatives, but always within the premise that every activity or ministry we began needed to have a missional meaning and to be accessible for the unchurched. It was a challenge to help Christians lose their 'churchiness' and live in a different way. Discipleship means calling people to live the 'Jesus way' not the 'Church way'. Over our years spent in church life we have often been painfully struck by the potential for time-wasting, or meetings lacking clear enough objectives and outcomes.

Today's young adults think about life differently. They are interested in a 'whole life' balance. Everything must be meaningful. This has tremendous potential in Christian discipleship. We need first to understand what they value and believe in. Then we may help them to align their values with the values of the kingdom of God.

Good leaders will want to work with this generation and bring out the best in them. There is no characteristic that cannot be channelled, challenged, changed, nurtured, developed by the Spirit of God (Rom. 12:2). This is what it means to be empowering leaders.

It is so important, for example, to realise that these generations have been raised to dream, and dream big. They are dreamers who are motivated by inspiration. They do not want to be managed, and much less told what to do or believe. They want to be led by leaders who create a culture where they may dream and run, providing them with support. Young adults around us at The Well Sheffield frequently ask the 'Why?' in relation to tasks or church structures. Outside of church, they are not used to simply being told 'it's this way'. As Generation X leaders, we have found it very important to understand the 'why' and work hard to answer it.

I am a whole person

Living purposefully and living in community are of utmost importance to this generation. If previous generations had a commitment to work and careers, this generation has a commitment to finding purpose in the whole of life. The whole of life matters and should be lived well. They are the generation that choose not to spend every waking hour in a corporate office to climb the career ladder. Being authentic means the same values find their expression in the office as in the café with friends. They have witnessed their parents' generation driven by performance or appearance at the expense of investing in their family and friendships.

This core belief in the integrated person is often misunderstood by older generations who perceive it as laziness and a lack of commitment. Millennials may be the first to leave their offices for an evening of socialising or exercise while their seniors work on and score points against each other for the long hours accrued at their desks. It would be a big mistake, however, to simply write this generation off as uncommitted. They are way more committed to causes than, for example, Generation X. Epitomised in individuals such as Malala Yousafzai, the Pakistani human rights activist and Nobel laureate, Generation Z have shocked the world as to how far they will go in commitment to a cause at such a young age.

Our opportunity is to help these generations realise that walking in the footsteps of Jesus will lead you to the most 'whole' kind of life. What does whole-life discipleship look like? Each of us needs to have a clear understanding if we are to spur one another on. If we can help the Church of today to live like Jesus in the whole of life, the kingdom will be breaking out all over the place. We need to articulate from the pulpit what discipleship according to Jesus looks like. We need to live it, model it and inspire it in others. It is a timeless message and the kind of life all are looking for. As we live it, others will follow.

When we were in our late twenties we were drawn to join and follow a local church minister in the adventure of the kingdom life and leadership. We could have chosen a number of people or teams to be a part of, but this man was unusual. He and his wife took deliberate journeys of faith and invited others to join them. For a season they lived in community with other young families; for a season they gave away their household salary and relied on God's weekly supernatural provision of food and money for their needs. At other times they opened their home weekly to pray for the sick. It was the radical Jesus-centred kind of life that we were longing for, and it was happening in our midst. As we joined in some of these faith adventures, we were dramatically shaped by the process. Looking back, we learned a lot of lessons, we made some mistakes, we gained a lot of wisdom and, most significantly, faith. Today, we hope that those we lead may see in us a similar lifestyle of faith adventure and become empowered to live that kind of way themselves.

I am more than a cog in a wheel

'Love each other. Just as I have loved you, you should love each other. Your love for one another will prove to the world that you are my disciples' said Jesus (John 13:34-35). Some of the language, tone and motives in church life can be slightly shocking. If vision is trumpeted ahead of culture being cultivated, then people can be viewed as useful commodities to achieving ministry goals, or as numbers in pews or figures in finance reports. This can seep in subtly but easily. Equally, in our homes today a vision for a teenager's life-goals can easily become all about achieving the highest exam grades. Of course, goals are helpful. But discipleship is about journeying with people in a spirit of love. People can be broken, messy, different and difficult at times!

Don't tell me what to do, but please introduce me to the wisest man who walked the planet

Jesus is many things to those who have a revelation of Him — He is Messiah, Saviour, Son of God, Friend of sinners. Yet, He is also Rabbi: a teacher to learn from through imitation. We often hear people say that this generation hates being told what to do, and yet they hold a deep longing for wisdom. One of the most effective ways to grow and empower disciples is not to tell people how we think they should lead their lives. It is rather in our teaching, training and preaching across churches that we paint a picture of Jesus, the wisest man to walk our planet.

During our years of ministry, we have tried to make the walk of a disciple as simple as possible as we teach and train new believers. During our twenties we were greatly impacted by the brilliant foundational teaching of Dallas Willard, who applied the Sermon on the Mount to contemporary life. He puts it simply. We are called to be with Jesus 'as one person to another, in our daily life'.[6] Apprentices or disciples then become capable of doing what their master does.

Willard says the 'how' of discipleship comes as we learn to 'Ask' to see Christ's reality, as we 'Dwell' in his word and 'Now Decide' to follow His ways.[7] This may be paraphrased to say that to be a disciple is to learn to:

Be with Jesus
Become like Jesus
Do the things that Jesus did.[8]

Throughout the Gospels, Jesus calls us to come, to be with Him, to follow Him, to be taught by Him and from that place to go and do the things He did. Dig into Matthew chapters 5, 7, 10 and 28 and it becomes very clear.

It is the abundant life (see John 10:10).

There is a way to live a 'whole life' and there is a narrow path to achieving it (Matt. 7:13). Few choose it. The danger is that many Christians in churches may miss it. But it is possible that these emerging generations, who question the meaning of everything, have a great chance to find it. The very traits which some find infuriating or baffling in Generations Y and Z may just be the greatest ingredients to finding and following the authentic paths of radical discipleship to Jesus.

Relationship and challenge

To anyone considering Jesus, He gives an invitation: 'come and see' (John 1:39). He appointed the twelve that they 'might be with Him' (Mark 3:14, NIV). In John 15 Jesus highlights that we cannot expect actually to live life and be fruitful 'apart from [Him]' (v. 5).

Jesus always invited people to follow Him. As they gained first-hand understanding of His values and lifestyle, He then challenged them to change, to 'take up [their] cross' (Matt. 10:38) and really begin to follow Him. This pattern of invitation and challenge must be navigated carefully. If we challenge people without a foundation of prior relationship, we can blow them out of the water and break down all trust and invitation to speak into their lives. Equally, if we are only ever full of affirmation and support for people but never tell them when we see something out of kilter, then we do them a disservice and will never truly disciple anyone. It requires pointing them to truth in the Scripture, asking reflective questions and bringing challenge. Jesus loved people really well, but He did not hold back from speaking truth to powers and offering people a better way to live. We must do the same.

We must walk this narrow path with caution. Today's dominant secular culture tends to see acceptance and affirmation as one and the same. There is a good deal of pressure to welcome people into church with a message that says, 'We affirm you as you are.' Yet Jesus always calls us towards change and transformation. This means that people need to hear God's truth and transforming grace spoken into their situations and mindsets. But a person can be quickly and deeply wounded when a word of challenge is delivered harshly or in a manner that prevents them from truly hearing the heart of what is being said. Instead, it is really important to build relationships; to take the time and care to appreciate, to hear and to understand a person, and for them to know that you are 'for' them. This atmosphere of high support creates the foundation of trust that allows us also to bring high challenge. This way, challenging conversations may happen 'in love' (Eph. 4:15) with Christ at the centre.

In our discipleship culture at The Well Sheffield, we emphasise that we should all ask and expect to be transformed by the power of God's Spirit. We do not expect anyone to be loved and affirmed by God simply to stay the same. There is always room for improvement. We describe it as 'Grace and Growth'.

This is very much a journey, not an overnight makeover. Sometimes we need to remind our young adults that joining a good church does not mean you will automatically become a disciple. Neither will all their issues be 'zapped' at the altar by the prayers of an anointed person with no effort on their part. Disciples are followers who are willing to lay down their lives.

We transition from being new believers having faith in Christ, to the faith 'of Christ' as disciples. Central to this is our understanding of our union with Christ. There is a journey to become Christ-like which is empowered by the spiritual reality that we already 'in Christ' (Gal. 2:16-20).

True transformation

Contemporary theologian and pastor John Mark Comer says, 'the first and primary goal of apprenticeship to Jesus is learning to live in a constant state of awareness of and connection to the Spirit.'[9] This principle may feel like an enormous challenge in the digital world in which we live. Our whole lifestyles and society seem to be set up to make this difficult. But we know it is possible with training, and most definitely worth the investment. As Brother Lawrence discovered 350 years ago at his kitchen sink, there is a whole new spiritual world available to those who learn who to practice the presence of God.[10]

> The first and most basic thing that we can and must do is to keep God before our minds . . . This is *the* fundamental secret of caring for our souls. Our part in thus practicing the presence of God is to direct and redirect our minds constantly to Him. In the early time of our practicing, we may well be challenged by our burdensome habits of dwelling on things less than God. But these are habits – not the law of gravity – and can be broken.
>
> (Dallas Willard, *The Great Omission*)[11]

As we spend time with our Master, we are naturally challenged to change. If we really encounter Him, nobody stays the same. We can only really change in response to Him. Human discipline or good ideas will not change us from the inside out.

The uncomfortable truth is that true transformation takes time and involves all of the following in work together: 1) Holy Spirit encounter 2) reading and hearing scripture 3) our effort 4) community 5) life's ups and downs. This kind of a life requires effort – lots of it, and no one can ever do it on their own. That is why we need each other and the different generations working together.

This is a truth we must faithfully proclaim and model, because it is not easily understood in this world of instant gratification and fast feedback. This book focuses on Generations Y and Z but it is clear that all individuals reach their potential when they realise they are part of a bigger picture. We are designed to be co-dependent, to honour and seek to empower each other, men and women alike. Sadly, this is not always how our institutions and societies operate but the most healthy cultures, whether in workplaces, homes or churches will reflect the example set in motion by Christ (1 Cor. 12:12-27). Likewise, generations reach their potential when valued and supported by the previous and emerging ones.

Genuine community

For a generation to thrive and for disciples to emerge there must be genuine community. Community does two things – it both exposes us and encourages us. Community is not the same as connectivity. In our increasingly connected digital age, loneliness continues to loom large. Nor is community the same as chemistry. Sometimes young adults join our church and describe to us the community they would like to join: 'I'd like to find a community with people aged between twenty-five to twenty-eight years, who like sport, live in this particular neighbourhood and who are free on Tuesdays, thank you!' What they really mean is: 'I would like to just mix with people like me! I would like to be with people who think like me; like what I like;

will tolerate me well.' This is chemistry, not community. It may make for great friendships but not true community.

Sadly, we meet many young people who wish to become Jesus' disciples but are honest enough to confess, 'We want the life but not the lifestyle.' Christian discipleship means being part of Christian community. True community occurs as a person shares who they are within a mix of different ages, different social classes, people not like you, people who parent differently, who vote differently, who share different views on life, whose children are annoying and so forth. When we share life around a common cause, these kinds of people will soften our sharp edges and challenge our natural assumptions so that we change for the better. They help me to become the best me.

Think of the early Church portrayed in Acts 13:1-3.[12] The church leadership team was made up of a young gung-ho Cypriot Jew (nicknamed Barny),[13] possibly two Africans (Simeon) and a travelling missionary and perhaps a Roman citizen from modern-day Libya (Lucius). Alongside them, a privileged Jewish childhood friend of the vasal governor (Manaen) and a former ultra-Pharisee once famous for his discriminatory religious terror (Saul). Together these teachers and prophets worshipped, fasted and sought the Lord's direction. What a racial, social and political mix! Yet, from this group in Antioch God was able to birth the first missionary journeys which were eventually to transform the Roman Empire.

Everyone is a missionary!

Disciples understand that to follow Christ means to point people to Him. In other words, everyone is a missionary commissioned to reach others with the good news.

Whatever your age, context, job: we are all missionaries. Yes you! It is not just for other people, or those called to other nations. Each Christian, or 'mini-Christ' is appointed to partake in the age-old mission of God to reach planet earth with the good news that there is a Father in the heavens who loves us, and makes a way for us to live and thrive in friendship with God. We are 'Christ's ambassadors' (2 Cor. 5:20).

We have found that the concept of being a 'missionary' does not come naturally to any generation. It requires brain-training to step into this identity in our everyday lives. For example, as a couple we define ourselves as being missionaries, not ministers. We are missionaries to the city of Sheffield. At almost every church service we tell stories and introduce and repeat the idea to our congregation that 'we are all missionaries' wherever we are, whatever our context.

The real deal

What does this mean for us? Well, in simple terms we might suggest it means to do the things Jesus did – and not a whole load of other stuff.

And to do *all* the things Jesus did – not just the parts we like.

As we develop discipleship in our different church and home contexts, it is vital that we are asking the question: does our discipleship look like discipleship according to Jesus?

> Go to . . . God's lost sheep. Go and announce to them that the Kingdom of Heaven is near. Heal the sick, raise the dead, cure those with leprosy, and cast out demons. Give as freely as you have received!
>
> *(Matt. 10:5-8)*

This is the normal Christian life. The most meaningful kind of life. 'Life in all its fullness' (John 10:10, GNT). Your own life, or those whom you are seeking to disciple in Jesus' ways, may not presently look like this. We encourage you to take a moment now to think about this, and what tweaks or changes might be necessary to move towards it.

Case Study:

Creating faith caps – an honest look at our lives

As we have journeyed through our married life, sometimes it has felt like we are leading a radical missionary life. At other times when we have taken a snapshot of our lives they have looked comfortable, middle class and not very different to everybody else's outside of the Christian world. It is then that we have learned the importance of intentionally creating faith gaps in our lifestyle, so as to allow enough space only for God to move. After all, if you want a life of miracles, you first have to *need* a miracle. For example, if we are in a place of security or financial abundance, perhaps it is time for us to give more money away? If we are in a time of enjoying the blessing of our nuclear family or holidays abroad, perhaps it is time to open up our home and family to others, to invite people to share food with us, live with us, or even go on holiday with us. Sometimes life naturally requires faith. Sometimes we need to deliberately leave enough of a gap that we can only live dependent upon God. This is the kind of life which requires us to walk in His grace, and see God come through for us.

Questions:

Where are you comfortable?
What needs to change?
What gaps can you help to create?

5. Dallas Willard, *The Divine Conspiracy* (London: Fount Paperbacks, 1998), p. 310.
6. Ibid., p. 303.
7. Ibid., pp. 323-326.
8. In particular, John Mark Comer has used this paraphrase, for example: https://bridgetown.church/practices/ (accessed 13.2.20).
9. John Mark Comer, *Practicing The Way*, Sermon ©Bridgetown Church 2016. www.practicingtheway.org/teaching/practicing-the-way [accessed 11.03.2020)
10. Brother Lawrence (Nicolas Herman of Lorraine, c.1614-91) was a layman who looked after the kitchen in a Paris Carmelite monastery. 'The time of business does not with me differ from the time of prayer; and in the noise and the clatter of my kitchen, while several persons are at the same time calling for different things, I possess God in as great tranquillity as if I were upon my knees before the Blessed Sacrament.' Brother Lawrence, The *Practice of the Presence of God* (London: Hodder & Stoughton, 2009).
11. Dallas Willard, *The Great Omission* (San Francisco, CA: HarperCollins, 2006), p.125.
12. Acts 13:1-3: 'Among the prophets and teachers of the church at Antioch of Syria were Barnabas, Simeon (called 'the black man'), Lucius (from Cyrene), Manaen (the childhood companion of King Herod Antipas), and Saul.' . . .
13. See Acts 4:36: 'For instance, there was Joseph, the one the apostles nicknamed Barnabas (which means 'Son of Encouragement'). He was from the tribe of Levi and came from the island of Cyprus.'

CHAPTER FOUR

This 'Unbelieving Generation'?

A generation ago in 1994 Grace Davie surveyed the cultural and religious landscape of Britain and declared the nation to be defined by 'believing without belonging'.[14] Official census or measurements of those regularly going to church had dropped massively since 1945 but she noted that 'the marked fall-off in religious attendance has not resulted, yet, in a parallel abdication of religious belief'. Britain could more accurately be described as an 'unchurched' rather than a 'secular' society.

Today, the figures tell the same story and it seems that spirituality is far from dead. Indeed, contemporary surveys suggest that openness to the supernatural is most alive within our youngest generations than any others, until people reach old age.

What is the UK picture of religion and faith among the young? A melee of colour and tone, a simultaneous paradox of Christianity, secularism and religious pluralism. Adherence to traditional religion is low, but there remains a clear consciousness of spirituality, and most young adults still act on this by doing things like praying – even without always being ready to identify where those prayers are landing.

A post-Christian generation

The British government's national census of 2011 reported a drop of 4.1 million in the number of Christians in England and Wales since the 2001 Census, especially among five to fourteen and thirty to thirty-nine-year-olds, despite overall population growth.[15] There is no doubt that religious affiliation has consistently dropped as the years have past. In 2001 30 per cent of fifteen to twenty-four-year-olds said 'Christian' in response to the question: 'What is your religion?' A decade later, it was 24 per cent.[16] There are big differences between the generations too: around two-thirds aged eighteen to thirty-four say they do not belong to a religion, compared to only one-third of the oldest age group. Attendance figures are similar, with around 40 per cent of over sixty-fives regularly attending religious meetings, compared with slightly more than 20 per cent of the youngest age group, eighteen to thirty-fours.[17]

There is another side to these statistics.

This may not represent the kind of decline we first imagine it to be. A very large 2017 UK survey showed that 51 per cent of the population identified themselves as 'Christian' while only 6 per cent of all adults (eighteen plus) identified as practising Christians.[18] Many people in our contemporary culture are spiritually attuned, they are looking for truth, they are seeking and will openly acknowledge a 'higher power' in the universe.[19] A close look at statistical surveys shows that the eighteen to thirty-four age group is often the most open to the possibility of the supernatural, open to prayer and being spiritual. They don't have a clear conception of Christianity, although they are rarely negative towards it. In fact, they tend to be more curious because Generation Z are now so post-Christian. There is a spiritual openness and hunger in Britain's unchurched generation.

There remains an inherited Christian identity deeply seated within British culture – just as in most European and Western nations. In the 2017 survey 85 per cent of respondents said they became Christians before age of eighteen, only 4 per cent between ages nineteen and thirty-four. This suggests that their affiliation to Christianity was rooted in their family, schooling, and inherited culture. Christianity remains firmly rooted within British identity, as it has been for 1,000 years, and still half of the UK population identifies with it personally.

Church affiliation is low but . . . faith may not be. In the same significant survey, representatives of the UK population were asked 'Would you call yourself a Christian who follows Jesus?' That is a black and white question. Twenty-eight per cent answered yes, 63 per cent said no. The highest percentage of YES was in the eighteen to thirty-five age bracket, the lowest percentage of NO was in the eighteen to thirty-five age bracket. Curiously, 9 per cent answered 'don't know' (highest within the eighteen to twenty-four age at 13 per cent). That may show a few things, like just how fluid ideas or beliefs are in the emerging generations – people are more comfortable holding to one view and then another in rapid succession.

This also reveals just how ignorant the rising generations are to the historic teachings and story of Christianity. It is no longer taught with any rigour in mainstream schools, it is largely derided by popular culture and portrayed in the media as irrelevant or even pernicious. That 9 per cent of the UK don't know whether or not they are actively following Jesus suggests that many people in the UK simply don't know who Jesus is, and what He represents.

In summary, a cultural sense of Christianity remains strong in the UK. That should spark a lot of hope in our hearts. The good news is that our emerging generations seem to view the residue of cultural Christianity in our European cultures as largely positive. Just over half of members of Generation Z (eighteen to twenty-four-year-olds) responding to a large survey said they had a positive experience of Christians/Christianity, even though two-thirds said they never went to church. Only 12-14 per cent of eighteen to thirty-fours felt that Christians were a negative force in society.[20]

What an opportunity

As we survey the landscape of contemporary Western nations, it could be easy to feel discouraged. Christian religious observance has fallen dramatically in recent decades as progressive society embraces multiple pathways towards human happiness. But what if we saw this as an opportunity, not a threat? This is a prime kingdom opportunity for believers who are willing to help point people towards an encounter with Jesus, the one true God. In a climate of believing without belonging, how can the Church reach and disciple those with an appetite for 'god'?[21]

'I do believe in the supernatural'

Why not see today's situation as exactly the space into which we can offer shape and form – the form of a cross-centred life – to open minds which are hungry for the supernatural?

A BBC survey[22] on attitudes to resurrection and life after death found that British adults are split equally among those who say they do (46 per cent) and do not (46 per cent) believe that there is life after death (i.e. reincarnation, heaven, hell). Once again, the highest proportion who 'do believe' were the twenty-five to thirty-four-year-olds.[23] Belief in miracles is high among Generation Z. When asked, 'Do you believe that miracles are possible today, or not?' 72 per cent of eighteen to twenty-fours said yes, making them the lowest age range to say no (26 per cent). Sometimes this belief translates into actions, with around 43 per cent having ever prayed for a miracle in any circumstance, and only 53 per cent saying no. This is reflected, or perhaps inspired, by US popular culture which in the past decade has seen a spike in TV shows such as *Supernatural* which completed its fifteenth season in 2020, or movies such as *It* which was remade in 2017.

Our timeless theology

The presence of God is the foundation and framework to any fruitful life. As Mark Sayers so aptly writes, 'Secularism is an attempt to create a system for human flourishing in which the presence of God is absent. As we explore the failings of the life system that secularism has created, we also see the damage that such an absence of God's presence creates.'[24]

All around us is a growing sense of dissatisfaction with Western life. There are endless opportunities to pursue pleasure, and yet people are deeply dissatisfied.

In the Garden of Eden God 'dwelt' amongst His people, and they walked in friendship with Him. After Adam and Eve ate from the tree of the knowledge of good and evil they were cut off from His presence (Gen. 2:16-18). This theme runs throughout Scripture and history. In the book of Exodus, we read of God's desire to dwell amongst the tribes of Israel (Exodus 25:8). Later God chose to allow His presence to dwell in the temple built by Solomon (1 Kings 8:10-11). However, years later because of the idolatry and sin of the people in Ezekiel chapters 8-11 we see that the presence of God was lifted from and left Solomon's temple. The glorious temple had been rebuilt by busy human hands yet the glory of the presence of God was absent. We know the end of the story: the promise of the New Jerusalem where the glory of His presence will cover the earth and again dwell with God's people (Revelation 21:2-3). In these in-between times, Jesus proclaimed that in Him is the redemptive promise that we may live with the presence of God today.

Anyone who believes in me may come and drink! For the Scriptures declare, 'Rivers of living water will flow from his heart.' (When he said 'living water,' he was speaking of the Spirit, who would be given to everyone believing in him. But the Spirit had not yet been given, because Jesus had not yet entered into his glory.)

(John 7:38-39)

The presence of God draws us back to friendship with our heavenly Father. We engage with the presence of God through the person of Jesus, His Word and Spirit. Make no mistake, in a confused, transitioning and increasingly secular society the presence of God becomes increasingly attractive. A nineteen-year-old male student recently came to our church. He had no memory of an experience of church, having not attended one since his childhood. At the end of the service he asked us if we thought it was possible that somebody would experience God's Spirit who had not yet decided that God was real. He asked the question because he realised it was happening to him! He returned a few days later to find out more and receive our gift of a Bible.

Case Study:

Spirit Café (www.spirit.cafe)

We have seen the reality of the nation's spiritual hunger and openness since we opened our Spirit Café at The Well Sheffield to the public on Friday nights.[25] Spirit Café is designed to reach those who are hungry to tap into something spiritual beyond themselves, though they may be confused about spiritual sources. Across the UK our pubs, festivals and fayres will host psychic, clairvoyant or other spiritual events which are very popular with the British public. We are confident and passionate that Christians should introduce spiritually hungry people to the presence, power and conviction of the Holy Spirit instead.

The Spirit Café model offers a menu of treatments written in a language designed to make sense to the unchurched. Visitors can ask for a 'Peace Treatment' or 'Spiritual Cleansing' which translates into prayer ministry from Spirit-filled Christians. As soon as people come through our doors, we are very clear that we are a Christian church and we will pray for them in the name of the Trinity: Father, Son and Holy Spirit.

Over the years we have seen many people from New Age backgrounds or other forms of spirituality such as Buddhism being drawn in to the café and also to the church. Some have gone on to become Christians, be baptised, and several have joined our School of Ministry. Many young adults also come who have not previously been spiritually searching. It is as if they become aware on the spot of their spiritual side and feel like a magnet is drawing them to desire an experience of God in that moment.

Jesus was generous with His ministry. He healed unbelievers,[26] He delivered Gentiles and Jews alike,[27] He was firstly concerned with demonstrating and proclaiming that they kingdom had come close to them – leaving them to make a personal decision about whether or not to follow Him further.[28]

A radical remnant

Christianity is now a non-mainstream identity in all Western nations outside the United States. Being a Christian is a conscious and alternative choice among all the generations. In some ways that creates a sense of isolation or incongruence with our progressive culture's prevailing norms. Yet because being a Christian is such a radical alternative, it also requires that our emerging adults take a stand to establish and model what living as a follower of Jesus must look like in the contemporary world. As one authoritative report puts it:

When they do not occupy an obviously dominant position in culturally and religiously diverse contemporary Britain, young Christians are obliged to reflect upon how to live out their religious identity. They wish to live out their beliefs authentically in everyday life, which involves 'being willing to stand up for their beliefs and speak up for social justice and accepting others without prejudice or reservation.[29]

There is now an opportunity for Christian nominalism to die, and what remains to be a more authentic expression of the Christian faith.

Jesus looked for spiritual hunger not religious observance

Causes are on the rise, a new kind of morality is replacing that of organised religion. People's spiritual hunger is real. Exploration and openness to the supernatural is exactly the kind of fertile soil for the gospel to be planted, and to flourish. This is just how Paul's missionary campaigns saw success in a polytheistic, sexually free first-century Europe.

In Jesus' eyes, what qualified people to receive the kingdom of heaven was very simple: faith. Just a glimmer of faith, a mustard seed.[30] Jesus was usually dismissive of those who kept up their religious observance without eyes and a heart to welcome the kingdom (John 9:39-41). But for those whose hearts and attention were sparked, to those with an attitude to seek out the spiritual treasure within Jesus – to those, Jesus gave abundantly. He said: 'Blessed are those who hunger and thirst for righteousness, for they will be filled' (Matt. 5:6, NIV). What a promise! You and I have an opportunity to help people to be spiritually filled, as we help them to journey towards Jesus.

The fields around us are 'ripe for harvest' (John 4:35), if only we have eyes to see it. The ground has shifted, but let us not assume it is purely a picture of religious decline into secularism, individualism or consumerism. The enduring characteristics which make us human remain in every generation – it is more a matter of their relocation. That means that Christians have the age-old missionary task of connecting the truth about Jesus to the cultural context of this moment. As Jesus pointed out, being spiritually hungry is one of the most important qualifiers for encountering God (Matt. 5:6).

Losing our religion: Changing our ways

Recently in our city we have witnessed many twenty-somethings coming to faith. The breakthrough came when they encountered and experienced the power and presence of God, through his Holy Spirit. We have devised various ways to help that happen, like our Spirit Café, street prayer ministry or Sunday services. Equally, we train and encourage our people to be willing and ready to pray for people or lead people into an encounter with God outside the boundaries of church. This could be at work, in gyms or cafés. We work hard to help people to drop their 'christianese' and use a language that is easy for the unchurched to understand, and to act as normally as possible, like praying for people with our eyes open. We have discovered that God is just as powerful at these times, and He loves to show up outside the church walls.

Usually we help to make a connection between the reality of Jesus and a person's inherent spiritual awareness, perhaps their sense of the supernatural or that feeling that 'there must be more'. Frequently the Gospels remark that 'when Jesus saw their faith'[31] He willingly extended His kingdom reach into their everyday reality. Faith, displayed in Jews and Gentiles alike, opened the door for people to be gifted physical healing, forgiven sins and salvation. Usually they did not have much of a clue who Jesus was before they encountered Him. They probably had poor doctrine and a mixed-up spirituality, but the hunger of faith within them was satisfied by the living God. As Jesus said when He sent out His followers to demonstrate and proclaim the good news in all the towns and villages, tell them, 'the Kingdom of God is near you' (Luke 10:9).

Strategies for evangelism

Here are five observations about how we might connect the gospel with those young adults who are spiritually open.

1. It is more about relationship than reason

Find ways to connect. There is no substitute for personal meaningful connection as a means to bridge gaps by genuinely hearing where others are coming from, and earning the right to share one's own story and spiritual world view. Contemporary studies show that the vast majority of young adults are favourable or vaguely neutral towards Christianity and our spirituality. Building connections and relationships will remove walls of ignorance. Most importantly, today's generations will not feel any need to give the Christian faith or you personally any hearing without some prior relational connection. Somebody's authenticity and integrity needs to be experienced, whether in person or via social media. It is no longer the case that a convincing argument will win over hearts and minds. Relationship is everything.

Here's what a 2019 Bible Society Report has to say:

If attitudes towards Christianity and the Bible are more neutral than negative, and the greatest barrier is apathy, might a different strategy for evangelism be needed? Whereas previous generations who harboured more questions and scepticism may have responded best to apologetics, the strategy for reaching an apathetic generation might be more about relationships than reason – non-Christians getting to know more Christians, on their own terms, and in their own context, outside of a church.[32]

2. Encounter and experience

Find ways that younger people can experience the spiritual truths we all hold dear. This is a 'show and tell' culture. People seek spiritual encounters, they are open to new experiences and will often prioritise things that appear enlightened, supernatural and that may generate positive feelings.

Sometimes we may need to lay aside our evangelical tendencies to present the gospel as a four-point argument that requires mental assent. Instead, give people a reason to wonder: could it be that there is a Father in the heavens who deeply loves me? It can look like drawing people into an encounter with God and then stepping back to allow God to have His way.

3. Spirituality on the streets

It is not by accident that initiatives such as Healing on the Streets[33] have taken off in recent years and are successful with the rising generations. Why should Christians keep prayer ministry to Sunday mornings at the front of church? Why not move ministry outside to where the people are? That is exactly what Jesus and the apostle Paul did (Acts 18:3). Let us have the confidence to seek to live out Jesus' instructions in Matthew 10:7-8: 'Go and announce to them that the Kingdom of Heaven is near. Heal the sick, raise the dead, cure those with leprosy, and cast out demons. Give as freely as you have received!'

At The Well Sheffield we endeavour several times per week to take different groups onto the streets to share our faith and the power of the Holy Spirit. These rhythms are a discipline, because without them nobody would make the time or have the courage to put them into practice. The leaders included!

4. Spirituality in the social

Christian spirituality needs to have relevance in the social space since this is the new arena of morality. In a culture which is cause-driven, where people are desperate to leave a legacy in life, the Jesus movement has a God-given opportunity to shine. We can have the greatest public confidence in the values of God's kingdom, such as justice, righteousness, hope, healing, wholeness, reconciliation and peace. This is a cause that we can call people into. Our public proclamations must show

how we connect the gospel to everyday society's hopes and fears. Our public proclamations must be backed up by genuine demonstrations of the gospel in action, with love not judgement in the social space.

5. Heritage is hip

Contemporary culture loves heritage and longevity. This is the reuse, renew, recycle generation. The UK Church has been around for hundreds of years, and you might be surprised to learn that most of our buildings are now considered as shabby chic. At The Well Sheffield many young adults have commented how much they love the pews and the simple stained glass in our 1905 stone building, beautifully complementing our bold contemporary café décor which they walk through upon entering. The Fusion student mission movement began using the #trychurch hashtag a few years ago, almost daring Generation Z to engage in an institution much older than themselves. Today's young adults are so unchurched that trying church is a novel experience, rather like trying a new cinema.

Conclusion: This 'unbelieving generation'?

Jesus decried His contemporary 'unbelieving generation' because they could not yet comprehend the implications of the Messiah in their midst (Mark 9:19). It was a lack of faith, not of belief. But with God, all things are possible (Matt. 19:26). Within that generation's lifespan the world saw the beginnings of a revival of faith which is still unfolding. Our God is all about redemption and reinvention and no culture is ever truly lost. Just as the missionaries of old, you and I have the opportunity to bring today's Generations Y and Z into a spiritual relationship with the living God.

In a society that holds to pluralism and no absolute truth, Generations Y and Z have many questions. Questions are good! We must never be afraid to allow people to ask questions in our desire for them to comprehend the truth. That is why programmes like the Alpha course and Christianity Explored have been effective for decades. They create a relational environment in which different opinions can be respected and individuals are supported in a journey towards God.

We are convinced that Jesus is no more disturbed or discouraged by today's social trends than He was of those pervading the Roman Empire 2,000 years ago. As the writer says, 'What has been will be again, what has been done will be done again; there is *nothing new under the sun*' (Eccl. 1:9, NIV). We can be confident that a lively Christian spirituality will always attract people towards God. Our missionary task is to make the connections very clear between our historic faith and contemporary practices. After all, 'the Church is called upon to proclaim afresh in each generation.'[34]

Case Study:

Student church planting – Alex Harris, Baptist minister, the Beacon Church, Stafford, UK

In February 2018 Keele University Christian Union organised a mission week and sought the support of local church leader Alex Harris. Although there were not many conversions during the week itself, hundreds of students did attend an event at which Alex spoke and hundreds expressed an interest in faith. It was clearly a move of God at a particular time and place. To respond to this, three courses called Christianity Explored were quickly begun, led by the students themselves between Easter and June. Interestingly, many of these young adults now say that over these three months many of them 'emerged' as Christians. They were unable to identify a specific day or event at which they made a conversion decision but rather, over time, they had become Christians while being saturated in the gospel message and gospel people.

By September 2018 after the summer vacation a church of more than 100 students had emerged on Keele campus, meeting in its chapel. This congregation would not see itself as part of Alex's local church, the Beacon, although they have drawn significantly on that church's resources and on relationship with Alex. This has required Alex to think of the priority of building towards God's kingdom, not simply His local church, and to invest his own time into raising incarnational student leaders in situ on campus.

To make the most of this opportunity, the Beacon Church have also bravely seen the priority of investing their resources of finance, staff and time in activities beyond themselves

14. Grace Davie, *Religion in Britain Since 1945: Believing Without Belonging* (Chichester: John Wiley & Sons, 1st Edition, 1994).
15. Peter Stokes, 'Full Story: What Does the Census tell us about religion in 2011'. Office for National Statistics. Available online: http://webarchive. nationalarchives. gov.

uk/20160108071649/http://www. ons. gov. uk/ons/dcp171776_310454. Pdf (2013) (accessed 6.12.19).

16. Rebecca Catto, 2014, 'What can we say about today's British religious young person? Findings from the AHRC/ESRC Religion and Society Programme', Religion, 44:1, 1-27, DOI: 10.1080/0048721X.2013.844740. https://www.tandfonline.com/doi/figure/10.1080/0048721X.2013.844740?scroll=top&needAccess=true# (accessed 6.12.19).

17. Lucy Lee, 2012, 'Religion: Losing Faith?' in eds. Alison Park et al, *British Social Attitudes: The 28th report.* 173–184. (London: SAGE Publications, 2012), p. 178.

18. Savanta ComRes, London, 2017. *Church of England Mapping Survey*, 12.09.2017. https://www.comresglobal.com/polls/church-of-england-mapping-survey (accessed 5.12.19).

19. A project investigating Christianity and the English university experience found 33 per cent said that they were 'not religious or spiritual' followed by 31 per cent 'not religious but spiritual', 2 per cent 'religious' and 11 per cent 'not sure'. Respondents were then asked: 'No matter how you have answered the previous question, to what religion or spiritual tradition do you currently belong?' In response 51 per cent percent chose 'Christian'.
Rebecca Catto, 2014, 'What can we say about today's British religious young person? Findings from the AHRC/ESRC Religion and Society Programme', Religion, 44:1, 1-27, DOI: 10.1080/0048721X.2013.844740. https://www.tandfonline.com/doi/figure/10.1080/0048721X.2013.844740?scroll=top&needAccess=true# (accessed 6.12.19).

20. Harriet Sherwood, 'Post-Millennial Generation 'More Tolerant' of Christianity', *The Guardian*, Guardian News and Media, 12 July 2018, www.theguardian.com/world/2018/jul/12/post-millennial-generation-uk-more-tolerant-of-christianity (accessed 6.12.19).

21. For example, the apostle Paul took careful note of the cultural, religious and philosophical context of Athens when we connected his one true God to the Athenians' altar to the 'Unknown God' as recorded in Acts 17:16-34.

22. Ibid. See endnote 18.

23. Only 85 per cent of active Christians in this category said they believe this.

24. Mark Sayers, *Reappearing Church* (Chicago, IL: Moody Publishers, 2019), p. 83.

25. This initiative is a member of the Spirit Café International network, begun by Laurie Arnott at Harvest Ministries in Birmingham, UK. www.spiritcafe.world.

26. John 9:35-38.

27. Matthew 15:21-28. The faith of a Gentile woman from the region of Tyre and Sidon obtains healing for her demon-possessed daughter.

28. For example, in Luke 17:11-19 Jesus healed ten lepers, one of whom was a Samaritan who returned to put his faith in Jesus.

29. Giselle Vincett, Elizabeth Olson, Peter Hopkins, Rachel Pain, 'Young People and Performance Christianity in Scotland', *Journal of Contemporary Religion* (2012) 27 (2) p282. Quoted in: 'What can we say about today's British religious young person? Findings from the AHRC/ESRC Religion and Society Programme' (2014). *Religion*, 44(1), 1–27. https://doi.org/10.1080/0048721X.2013.844740 (accessed 5.12.19).

30. See Matthew 17:20.

31. For example, Mark 2:5, NIV.

32. Rachel Rounds, 'Digital Millennials and the Bible.' *Bible Society*, Bible Society, 2018, p. 22. www.biblesociety.org.uk/latest/news/digital-millennials-and-the-bible/ (accessed 6.12.19).

33. For more see www.healingonthestreets.com

34. The Preface to the Declaration of Ascent of Church of England Deacons, Priests and Bishops. 'The Declaration of Assent', ©The Archbishop's Council 2007, Church House Publishing, www.churchofengland.org/prayer-and-worship/worship-texts-and-resources/common-worship/ministry/declaration-assent (accessed 6.12.19).

CHAPTER FIVE

Mentoring Matters

Recently at a wedding reception we sat around a large table with five beautiful-looking young adult couples. All had married within the past two years, and we had prepared four of the couples for marriage, as well as playing a role in their wedding ceremonies. It was a joy to spend hours with them laughing, listening, learning and reminiscing. As the conversations deepened, one couple shared how the past couple of years had not always been easy for them and how grateful they were for our preparation and wisdom along the way. 'I always remember Marjorie saying, "When you marry, you marry for life. That is what we are preparing you for."' This young man was not the only one at that table who shared how much they had appreciated the input of older adults who were further along the journey of marriage. It was so encouraging for us to hear their different stories and to be reminded of the privilege it is to invest into others' lives. We realised that some of our input makes a difference, at least some of the time!

Emerging adulthood is *not* just an extension of adolescence. It is a transitional season of life which is best aided by the scaffolding of ongoing support and advice from parents/family and institutions such as university or work. In Sheffield we are regularly asked by young adults to help them find a mentor. The Church is the greatest cross-cultural, cross-generational body on earth, and is therefore best placed to apprentice young adults into a lifestyle and mindset which mirrors Jesus. The purpose of Christian discipleship is to empower emerging adults to:

- Discover their present purpose within the big story of God – to 'seek the Kingdom of God above all else, and live righteously'.[35]

- Discover and live from their adult identity

- Navigate their choices with discernment

In everyday life, or in the weekly activities of a local church, discipleship occurs through a series of deliberate small steps. A framework is helpful, but it would be a mistake to think of discipleship in terms of schools, programmes or courses. More often than not it happens in the nitty-gritty and the normal. Apprenticeship occurs when those more experienced, and usually older, intentionally and honestly share their journey, including what they've done well and what they've done wrong. As the master-craftsman and apostle Paul wrote to his own mentee Timothy, 'imitate me . . . as I imitate Christ' (1 Cor. 11:1).

Will today's older generations within the Church be willing to adapt in order to raise the next generation of disciples in this way? Will local church leaders help to identify the best mentors and create those connections?

What a remarkable opportunity we have to connect the generations within the safety of a local church family who share values, passion and purpose. Young adults delight in finding people who believe in them, so that they can believe in themselves. They will actively seek out the wisdom and friendships of older generations. This is very different from Generation X who were rather anaemic or cynical towards their elders and wanted to separate themselves to do and proudly discover a 'new thing'. It is different now. In the Allan household, our teenage daughter is constantly on the phone to both her grannies, talking through life's choices and challenges.

Generations Y and Z actually expect and long for regular feedback, and they respond really positively to encouragement. They are used to constant evaluations and appraisals in their different learning contexts. In terms of discipleship, the door to hearts is wide open if you are willing to give them your time and thoughts. This is why all of us older generations can play a part in supporting and loving the young around us. Nobody is discounted from this.

Navigate alongside

Young adults seek this kind of connection, stories and wisdom – not necessarily because they feel they are *sinking*, but because they recognise they need assistance in *navigating* these uncharted waters of emerging adulthood. Authors Dunn and Sundene, who are spirituality specialists, offer an excellent outline of what this can look like for mentors:

> effective spiritual guides for emerging adults spend time building spiritual friendships and discerning appropriate direction and then move in caring, responsive, intentional ways to help other navigate the uncharted waters of their faith journey. They hike alongside others in suffering, celebration and all that lies between, helping to identify the work of the Holy Spirit in the ups and downs of everyday circumstances and decisions. Effective disciple-makers also purposefully explore the deep truths of the faith *with* emerging adults rather than *parallel* to them. Finally, an effective spiritual caregiver takes time to reflect and re-evaluate as the path unwinds.[36]

This kind of approach is not as easy as it sounds. When interacting with young adults, it is often tempting to want to offer a lot of advice, or to point out the pitfalls you can predict further down some particular paths. But the way to connect best with Generations Y and Z is more to embark upon a journey of mutual discovery, since they are rather resistant to the kind of advice or wisdom that feels like it is 'unearned' and just dropped in from above. They will be looking for the authenticity of your life. In our experience, they will ask, 'Does this work in real life?' or, 'Has this person actually experienced what they are talking to me about?' The vein of individualism runs deep in these generations, and on the whole they will want to make their own discoveries, and their own mistakes. In his 2016 thesis research into how UK university graduates seek and find belonging in new church communities, Matthew Ward includes a very instructive quote from one young man. Oliver was passionate about social justice, but he wanted to explore the topic on his own terms, rather than at the direction of others.

> I want to follow my own individual path, want to travel as a discoverer not as a package holiday tourist who is being shown around. Sometimes, I will appreciate that someone can tell me that he or she has already been to the same place and had this or that experience but, in the end, I want to wander around on my own guided by my thoughts and conscience.[37]

Does the local church help or hinder?

The question comes as to whether the local church is making the most of this opportunity? Faith communities over the centuries have introduced intentional patterns to make the most of mentoring, from the oikos households of faith in the early Church, to monastic communities or Wesleyan class discipleship groups. Has that inter-generational passing-on of experience dropped out of local church behaviour?

Some of our current patterns may not help. Perhaps we are too focused on Sunday services which are public, sometimes formal and impersonal and only allow for the lightest of social interaction in a few minutes before/afterwards. Are there deliberate opportunities for the generations to interact? Are we inviting younger people into discipleship groups with agreed intentions and parameters (not just Bible studies)? Are we arranging to meet over a coffee?

Mothers and fathers in Christ

The Church is a spiritual family and our connection to each other is like a body (1 Cor. 12:12-27). Our interaction with others was never intended to be transactional, based on what I can do, or my hierarchical position – it is always relational. For some mentors that means not simply that you will be a source of good advice or even good company, but that you should become like a spiritual mum or dad to one or two younger adults. Maybe for a season, maybe for many years while they mature and become ready to do the same with the generations who will follow them. What does it mean to be a spiritual parent to somebody?

> For even if you had ten thousand others to teach you about Christ, you have only one spiritual father. For I became your father in Christ Jesus when I preached the Good News to you.
>
> *(Paul to the church in Corinth, 1 Cor. 4:15)*

Paul describes two very significant roles here. The 'teachers' about Christ are *paidagōgós* in Greek, which refers to a tutor of boys, an appointed overseer whose role in ancient times was 'authorized to train (bring) up a child by administering discipline, chastisement, and instruction'.[38] It has the idea of a rather stern enforcer, and the word is also used of the role of the Old Testament Law in laying proper foundations and morality. But it is not a warm or nurturing word, it is a necessary function. Every new Christian or young person needs to know the boundaries and foundations of the Christian life and have people to bounce off as they test some of those boundaries. But Paul goes on to describe an all-the-more powerful role of *patér* – a father, a life-giver who is all about intimacy and relationship, a nourisher, protector, upholder.[39] It is how Jesus describes His Father God (Matt. 6), it is how Paul sees himself in relation to Timothy whom he calls 'my . . . son' (1 Tim. 1:2). Mothering and fathering believers in the faith, in life and leadership is the picture we see throughout the New Testament and among those Christian communities who have taken discipleship seriously over the years.

A generosity of heart is required for this role as well as a secure identity. The more secure we are in our own identity in Christ, the more we are free to love and invest in others with no personal agenda – so that when your mentee messes up or rejects us and/or our wise advice, or simply makes different choices to you, we may remain safe in the knowledge that whatever happens, we are never failures and we have no need to be insecure or to prove ourselves to others. Secure mothers and fathers can expect their spiritual children to have alternative ideas from them, to do things different or better; in short, to do things their way. The most mature parents will seek to install a family likeness of Christ-like living and Christian faith, and after that they will refuse to be afraid of letting their mentees have a good go and develop their own expressions. It is not about 'mothering them along' – it is about empowering them to mature, at which time we will more than likely need to release them from being our 'spiritual children' in order that they may fully mature, fly the nest, and repeat the process with others in future.

Case Study:

The life-cycle of a mentoring relationship

When we were leading our first church, a couple in their mid-twenties felt God call them to move to our city, to commit to our church and to support the Allans as a family.

They were a gift from God to us during a very fruitful and very intense period of ministry as our family grew to three young children. He sent us two Spirit-filled, faith-filled friends who were mature beyond their years. We invested into them as much as possible. They were frequently in our home, we ate together, worshipped and served together and as our Sunday responsibilities expanded, they became surrogate parents at times to our children. The young man became our first ministry intern so that we could help him to navigate his Christian leadership and ministry calling. The young lady would chat for hours with Marjorie as we shared everyday life.

It was a mentoring relationship, but very much a two-way experience. As much as we spoke into their lives and helped them to make decisions, we also learned a tremendous amount from this wise and humble couple who encouraged us into new levels of love and devotion to Jesus. Their biblical insight and radical service fed our souls, while we were able to feed theirs.

As the years passed, we each grew in our faith, skills, capacity and life responsibilities. Both parties recognised that this couple who began as a spiritual son and daughter in a mentoring relationship had now reached a maturity in faith and in life. It came time for them to move away from our city for new jobs and to follow God's call. Together we had a conversation about it and mutually and quite formally recognised that this marked the end of that period of our mentoring relationship. It was time for them to 'leave home' metaphorically and change the way they related to us. From now on it was to be as adult-adult. The Allans blessed and released them. They blessed and thanked us. It was emotional and a very healthy step to take. Today this couple remain our dear friends, and Godparents to our youngest child.

What young adults are looking for

Leaders are not placed on pedestals any longer. These younger generations long and look for authenticity. Twenty years ago, our Generation X valued a stable leader who led with authority and vision with an ability to steer the ship. Leaders' lives were often somewhat removed from everyone else, church pastors remained 'six foot above contradiction'. Particularly in large church contexts, senior leaders were often somewhat inaccessible, they led busy lives and you booked appointments to see them.

There has been a huge shift over the last decade in the average British workplace in line with a general erosion of hierarchical markers within progressive Western society. Society and educational structures have so distinctly changed that very few organisations operate today with a top-down leadership paradigm. In general, most of today's young workforce have an expectation that things will happen in a collaborative way. This way of thinking and working develops many years earlier in the way in which group work is now encouraged from primary school age. Ideas are shared, people must learn to value and respect each other in teams, all viewpoints get to be heard and the best ideas win.

This expectation within Generations Y and Z can mean they are seen as being not very respectful of their leadership. They are not trying to appear arrogant; they are simply reflecting how their elders have brought them up to value independent thought. Sometimes this applies just as much in a church setting. If we respond like an expert, we risk losing their attention and trust very quickly. Recently a senior national Baptist leader shared with me their surprise and amusement at how the younger generation think nothing of contacting them directly and instantly, via FaceTime or sending them repeated direct messages. They obviously see their seniors as far more accessible than previous generations ever did. In fact, they may recognise them as senior, but not necessarily superior, in other ways. There is little intimidation or formality that restricts them from simply approaching a leader (or lecturer, or employer) upfront with no introduction.

In today's culture, leaders are respected who openly acknowledge their weakness but are willing to work through them. It means that in our public teaching and interactions it is absolutely vital, whether in small or large contexts, that we are honest and willing to be real. Those who do this will have the privilege of being invited to disciple this generation.

Authenticity and vulnerability

Sometimes we, the Allans, have to hold our tongues when a young adult challenges us or shares their opinion on something we have just preached. We may have spent many hours researching and preparing the talk, yet they see their immediate reaction/view as equally valid to ours. At times like this we have to smile in response and swallow our generational small-mindedness. It is so wonderful that Generations Y and Z have the buy-in and hunger to be present and want to ask these questions and think for themselves.

In the 1990s, our employers would give us formal feedback about once a year, usually from one senior manager. Today's generations are raised in a context where feedback on performance happens from anyone at any time, and a world in which good ideas come no longer from a carefully selected group of experienced individuals, experts or teachers. It means people are more likely to express an opinion, come up with a creative idea and take ownership. Generations Y and Z are confident when leading up, as well as leading across or down.

More than ever before, leadership is influence, far more than being conferred by title or position. Some of our culture's most influential voices come from our social media, dominated by celebrities. A few young adults told us recently that they are swayed to vote in our political elections for whoever their favourite celebrity endorses.

Appropriate disclosure

Authenticity does not mean that we need to look the same or even have the same values as those we mentor. But it does mean we need to walk the talk. It is important to understand what vulnerability looks like. It does not mean that we must be emotionally driven as leaders or are inappropriately open. It does not mean we are crippled by fear or lack faith. But it does mean we can show our human side, recognise weakness, share hardships. It means we must be honest. When Nick was first at theological college in the early 2000s 'appropriate disclosure' in pastoral care was encouraged: sharing enough of one's personal challenges to encourage those you care for to do the same. Today it is not only 'appropriate', it is a necessity if leaders and mentors are to connect with Generations Y and Z.

Today's young adults are seeking the wisdom of people willing to act as enablers, not experts. Humility is so important. As one practitioner eloquently put it, 'This generation don't want a "sage on the stage", they're looking for a "guide by their side".'[40]

'I'm not being rebellious when I ask, "Why?"'

As we mentor, it is helpful to have a grid for conversations and questions. Simple discipleship creates a space for someone to ask 'What is God saying to me?' and follow it with 'And what will I do about it?'

Do not be intimidated as Generations Y and Z ask you a heap of questions. 'Why?' from this generation may be asked from a different heart than we may first imagine. It felt like rebellion for the Boomer generation (born approx. 1946-64) to question 'Why?' to those in authority, or a lack of commitment or loyalty.

To Generation X it often came out of a cynical heart. 'Why?' to a Millennial is often a general quest for information rather than a judgement upon those in authority.

Being a good mentor or discipler does not mean that you lay aside your common sense, good judgement or, indeed, your opinions or values. It means you share them carefully with permission, with enough 'Why?' and a listening ear. And by listening, it helps to remember we do not just mean listening and then immediately discounting a person's views/ideas/opinions. It means really listening with an open mind and a heart to hear and understand. It is frighteningly easy for any generation to be dismissive of another because of their preconceived notions, but that is frighteningly dangerous, because we all only see 'in part' (1 Cor. 13:9,12, NIV).

Perhaps a good, safe starting point is to focus on the listening, not the telling. A mentor who asks open-ended questions, listens to the responses and steers people towards Scripture and the fruit of their considered opinion is worth gold.

Mentoring methods

In the feedback culture in which Millennials have been raised, they will greatly appreciate your intentions to encourage a rhythm of intentional reflection and your desire as a mentor for them to grow in self-awareness and personal insight. Most people find it hard to identify one's hidden self: those motivations (good or bad) which drive us from deep within. Mentors can help a person to dig deeper, to interrogate their inner beliefs, past experiences or inherited views and values which help to form their world view and motivate their actions. Sometimes it is more helpful to stop and ask why something has happened before we help a person to answer, 'What next?' Use open-ended questions like 'Why, when, where, how . . .?' because most people can be almost unaware of their internal drivers or shadow side without external help.

Mentors have an open invitation which means, unlike a secular counsellor, that you do not need always to remain detached, value-free and not sharing an opinion. We are invited to help set the kingdom of God values and world view as the foundation. The aim is to empower our mentee to learn to discern.

Are you open-minded enough to help me?

As we reflect over our lives, we are grateful for the wise people who cared enough to speak truth to us and highlight areas of our lives or thought patterns where we were short-sighted or blind. The best mentoring is not what a young person might expect or even appreciate sometimes. It is not simply allowing them to express and acknowledge the emotions which are raised in response to events. It is enabling them to process and reflect on events or feelings. This allows for somebody to take responsibility and make changes. It does not mean that you have to become inclusive of their views at the expense of your values. It means that you are open-minded enough to handle doubt, fears, insecurities, unfinished viewpoints and a lack of self-awareness that are typical in this age group. We handle them with grace and wisdom: with a mentor's guidance, not a schoolmaster's discipline or disappointment.

In the Gospels, Jesus was not fully affirming of anybody's lifestyle or decisions. He always offered a mixture of grace and growth, of invitation and challenge. To a range of people He says, 'Neither do I [condemn you]. Go and sin no more' (John 8:11); 'If you want to be perfect, go and sell all your possessions and give the money to the poor, and you will have treasure in heaven. Then come, follow me' (Matt. 19:21). Mentors should offer a mixture of care, encouragement and help to celebrate the little and the big. We should not be afraid to challenge ungodly and immature stances so that 'we will speak the truth in love, growing in every way more and more like Christ' (Eph. 4:15).

A 2018 report into raising Christian Millennials into workplace leadership put it well:

> Create environments of high support and high challenge where millennial leaders can take risks, experiment, fail, pick themselves up again, be encouraged, and develop and grow. The proximity to leaders' lives being encouraged within these cultures means they are highly attractive to millennials because they can observe other leaders up close, ensure their own words and actions align in a highly practical way, and be part of a supportive team. One church leader talked of creating 'huddles' for leaders across all sectors of society that met fortnightly, enabling them to tackle real life issues in a supportive environment.[41]

Not one size fits all

Let us not be too prescriptive in our models or advice. There is never a one size fits all. There are usually nuances to be found. Perhaps many of us over the years have experienced organised Bible studies which, although very well-intentioned, are so generic in their approach to discipleship or application of Scripture that they fail to scratch deep enough below the surface of our lives. Perhaps you can picture the scene of young adults who are being discipled by their slightly older peers. The person assigned to them, perhaps a young adult or student worker or a small-group leader, keeps ploughing methodically through chapters of a workbook. They read a passage, they discuss its application but . . . not really. Because it tends to remain exclusively cerebral and 'in theory'. The younger mentee might manage to answer a few questions 'correctly', or sometimes they have very little to offer until their mentor steps in with some generic wisdom from the pages of their book.

While you might argue that it is of great value to train young adults to read the Scripture, this approach is not individualised or contextualised. Getting the answers 'right' to a theoretical (and perfectly doctrinally correct) set of 'thou shalts' usually results in missing the opportunity to dig into and hear a person's deepest motivations or opinions. They never get around to asking the questions which unlock the soul and challenge the character.

I may fail, but I'm not a failure

A good mentor is there for you the day you get it wrong and it feels like failure. We can really help this generation to take risks and process their disappointments. The grace in that experience is the gospel message that people themselves are never failures. I may fail, but in God's eyes I am never a failure. This is important for people's self-esteem and self-belief: it actually helps to root belief into the works and person of Jesus instead.

Our experience is that Generation Y can find situations of conflict to be very challenging because their first reaction is often avoidance. Similarly, they can struggle to dig in and walk through situations of trial or personal denial. Never before has life been so convenient. You can order an instant pizza, an ironed shirt or a recreational sex partner all with the click of an app on your mobile phone. In this world of the constant and the instant, patience and perseverance are not prized. For those of us who are Gen X or older generations, we have a lot to offer in drawing alongside the young around us and encouraging them to make wise choices for the long-term and, above all, to keep going. As we draw alongside others who find themselves in the deep valleys of life, the counsel we repeatedly give is: 'Don't sit down in that valley. Keep going!' This comes with the wisdom of years, since we know that eventually most people will walk out of their valleys towards new mountaintops. As the apostle Paul who knew so much suffering encourages us, 'endurance develops strength of character, and character strengthens our confident hope of salvation' (Rom. 5:4). This is possible when we become rooted in our identity in Christ which also grows over time, as does the inner transformative work of the Holy Spirit.

Safe spaces

Sadly, by the time many people reach their early twenties, they will have experienced abuse of some kind. Often this is accompanied by the reaction or coping mechanism of depression or suppression of emotions. We have numbers of university students in our city, and each year we see rising instances of the disclosure of abuse. This is no longer a surprise to us, although it is always a tragedy.

Church ministries should expect to encounter this increasingly into the future. Alongside ensuring we have robust safeguarding procedures we can help by creating 'safe spaces' where people feel unjudged and cared for enough to open up. 'Safe Spaces' is now a common term within education context – why not within church? At The Well Sheffield we address some issues publicly and others in private. Every year we run public seminars on topics including relationships and how to relate well to others; dating; marriage; singleness. We run an annual course written by Christian medical experts addressing common mental health and wholeness questions, seeking to build resilience in people towards a whole-life balance.

True transformation

In mentoring and discipleship, we seek to move people beyond their present position. A safe space means that people take time to acknowledge and be supported within their present pain. But the beauty of Christian community allows for us to expect that people may be empowered by the Holy Spirit and the love of others to move forward again and to experience the freedom of Christ. We do not have to be perfect before we attempt to live for God as disciples in the everyday. Occasionally churches should offer well-trained people to walk with hurting young adults into prayer ministry, inner healing and occasionally by prior agreement, in deliverance. Do not discount the power of simple prayer ministry response times at public events like church services: the opportunity to come alongside somebody and to bless what God is already doing. However, some circumstances may be very complex so at times the local church will need to encourage individuals to seek professional advice or counselling elsewhere.

Case Study:

Nathan (age twenty-six)

Practical tip to my fellow Millennials. Seek advice from godly people but ... seek advice from God above all else. Older people have more life experience. *Fact.* God has more experience and life than anyone else. *Fact.*

If we are to create mature disciples, they need to learn how to learn (ironic, I know). To humble ourselves and seek advice from people who have been on similar journey and are more mature is biblical and just incredibly helpful. Countless times God has placed older people around me to counsel, support, laugh and even cry with me over situations. We are all in the same boat together in life, we are all trying to survive. Let's help each other do it. Let's be 'slow to speak', 'quick to listen' and quick to love.[42] As a church and faith, we are all about empowering and supporting people through their oppression and depression.

However, empowering does not mean protecting young adults from issues and consequences. A lot of damage can be done by the concept of 'helicopter' parenting/ mentoring. Taking on other's issues, instructing and trying to protect them can be detrimental and stunting to growth and maturity. Many times, people go in with the best intentions but can hinder what God is doing. I know in my own life, one of the hardest, yet most liberating lessons came from defying my parents about a job that had come up. God told me one thing, my parents told me another. I listened to my heavenly Father, didn't go for the job and learned an important lesson: my faith is between me and God. Others can only advise, but the final word comes from the Lord. Others can only influence, but I now know my faith is based around my love for Jesus, not my parents or any other persons. Our learning is to listen to Him.

Spiritual sons and daughters become fathers and mothers

When all is said and done, a person's faith is based in their relationship with God, and in who we know Him to be. Faith can be caught and taught from others around us, but it can only be grown and established individually. It is very natural for young people's faith to be strongly influenced and nurtured by those around them – this is a good thing; whether that is youth and church leaders, peers, or mature Christians. Sometimes today's emerging generation is described as 'the kids who don't want to grow up'. As we mentor and invest into these generations, we must be careful that we do not feed this tendency in an unhealthy way. Faith must be tested and owned by each one. 'These trials will show that your faith is genuine. It is being tested as fire tests and purifies gold' (1 Pet. 1:7). Let us raise a generation of sons and daughters who are empowered, regardless of age, to know that their true identity is solely rooted in God. In time they will mature to become spiritual mothers and fathers to others. This is essential to the health and vitality of the local church.

THE XYZ OF DESCIPLESHIP

Let them grow up

Finally, a word about our own identities and motivations as we seek to mentor others.

Remember our purpose is to raise disciples who go on to raise more disciples. Let us never become self-serving. There is always the potential that we mentor or advise ultimately for *our* sake, not the other person's. That we are too prescriptive in our models or advice simply because we only see 'in part' (1 Cor. 13:9,12, NIV). We need to be self-aware and generous enough that we avoid helping those we mentor to make decisions which ultimately serve *our* agenda – like serving more in church, or joining my internship, or living close to home ...

It is the Holy Spirit of God who really guides and disciples – we just help, and try not to get in the way! We are discipling people into faith and freedom, so they may be empowered to change their culture and cities, not just to serve the church, and certainly not to serve us.

35. Matthew 6:33.
36. Richard Dunn and Jana L. Sundene, *Shaping the Journey of Emerging Adults* (Downers Grove, IL: IVP, 2012), p. 77.
37. Matthew Alan James Ward, 'Searching for belonging: an exploration of how recent university graduates seek and find belonging in new church communities' (Durham theses, Durham University, 2016), p. 106. Available at Durham E-Theses Online: http://etheses.dur.ac.uk/11825/ (accessed 5.12.19).
38. Strong's Concordance, '3807. Paidagógos'. *Strong's Greek: 3807. Παιδαγωγός (Paidagógos)*, Biblehub, www.biblehub.com/greek/3807.htm (accessed 5.12.19).
39. Strong's Concordance. '3962. patér.' *Strong's Greek: 3962*. πατήρ (patér), Biblehub, www.biblehub.com/greek/3962.htm (accessed 5.12.19).
40. Baptists Together National Mission Forum, *Young Adults 18-35s and the Church* (Didcot: Baptist Union of Great Britain, 2019), unpublished report, p. 4.
41. Forge Leadership Consultancy, *Millennial Leaders: Now is Our Time and this is Our Voice* (London: Forge Leadership Consultancy, 2018), p. 36.
42. See James 1:19.

SECTION TWO

Discovering Our Identity

technology has shaped their thinking, facilitated communication, redefined community, affected their sense of identity, influenced their consumer preferences and become core to their learning and like a constant companion to them.[43]

Claire Madden, *Vogue Australia*

43. Claire Madden, 'Move over Millennials: Everything to Know about Gen Z', Vogue Australia, ©NewsLifeMedia 24 November 2019, www.vogue.com.au/culture/features/move-over-millennials-everything-to-know-about-gen-z/news-story/2ddef9cb4ff31b7b4934454a002676cf (accessed 5.12.19). This article originally appeared in Vogue Australia's July 2019 issue.

CHAPTER SIX

Who Am I in the Age of the Selfie?

Identity 1

Identity is the foundation to everything.

It is unusual to find a young person today who does not live with their phone in hand, constantly delving into what is not just a 'world of others' but a very real extension of their own world. They are permanently plotting their updates so as to present a carefully crafted image. Instagram, TikTok, Facebook, Snapchat: today any number of apps are at hand not only to present a life story to a waiting world, but to edit, to manipulate, to curate content so that people really can 'put on their best face'. Never before has a generation been so keen to project a public image or persona and to keep up with changing trends. This is a world defined by ratings, the TripAdvisor of our own lives.

It might also be true to say we live in an age where the self is king. Self-centred is no longer a pejorative term but a reality. People give an account of their life, posing with their face at the centre. Today's tourists do not just take photos of famous locations, they ensure their record of the Eiffel Tower or the Grand Canyon has their face alongside it, captured brilliantly by the selfie stick. If Generation Y grew up shaped by the selfie, Generation Z are growing up admiring the 'instafamous', and many desire to reach that level of fame themselves. They are creating online followings and even enlisting sponsorships to do so.

Our photos, videos and records of daily life and adventures are, of course, generally accompanied by short statements of opinion. In the world of social media, our opinions are everything. It is often the case now that one's views and opinions are no longer shaped by abstract truth, they are shaped by oneself – by our experience.

Discipleship is all about dethroning ourselves and discovering the reality that no, we are not God! The sooner we do this, life naturally works better. But we would be foolish not to realise that in today's celebrity culture the cross-carrying lifestyle is so completely countercultural. As followers of Christ, whatever the generation, we find our true sense of identity as we discover who God is. That is practical theology. If we have truly died to our old selves and are now 'hidden with Christ in God' (Col. 3:3), then any attempt to find ourselves outside of the identity of the Trinity will lead us down futile paths.

On and offline

Jesus had a strong sense of identity. He lived authentically to a truth about himself, His identity. Identity is the core truth you believe about yourself – so it determines how you live your life. This is because almost all of your actions follow your sense of identity. We act in a way consistent with what we believe about ourselves and about the world around us. Jesus lived from a core truth that He was deeply loved by His heavenly Father. He walked with those words which thundered out at His baptism ringing in His ears: 'This is my Son . . . with him I am well pleased' (Matt. 3:17, NIV).

In this world where we carry a public persona which is often somewhat at odds with our life offline, we are in danger of projecting a lie, or of being conflicted and feeling at odds with the image we carefully curate for the watching world.

If you ask young adults about their life online, they will probably admit with sadness that social media tends to encourage them to project a fake personality. For example, they might post a photo of themselves surrounded by people, while in reality feeling that they had few friends and often feel isolated and lonely. Seeing similar posts from others only confounds these sentiments of feeling alone. How ironic, since these online community tools are heralded as enabling connection like never before. Connection, yes. But it is often on the basis of sharing information, rather than authentic collaboration, which is the glue of genuine community life.

A recent documentary about social media lifted the lid on the mental health effects of both being a vlogger (producing and posting videos of your daily life) and constantly viewing the lives of others. The researchers commented that we are playing with something we do not yet fully understand. The long-term mental and emotional side effects of curating an online persona, and fishing for 'likes' and positive comments, are yet to be fully measured. It will be in the decades to come that we see the long-term effects of this lifestyle, but it is already clear that those whose life revolves around public posts online are usually crippled by anxiety offline. The validation, for example, they received from a post or video gave them an adrenalin high such as any drug or release of endorphins would do.

But this thirst for validation does not build a healthy self-esteem. YouTubers would be the first to admit that social media is no loyal friend. It is fickle. 'Likes' or views can drop dramatically overnight, and negative 'trollers' can twist viewers' perceptions. This can have a powerful effect on those people who create content, as they find that their sense of esteem and self-worth rise or fall in relation to how their online presence is performing. It is near impossible not to live lives of comparison and judgement of others. This can seriously weaken people's sense of security around body image, success and positive achievements in life. As a result of this social whirlwind, many young people are quick to make a self-diagnosis that they are suffering from social anxiety disorder or depression.

Undoubtedly individual identity confusion is compounded by society's confusion at large, and the potential damage upon the mental health of a generation is frightening. The Church must rise and take responsibility to raise a generation confident in their identity based in how Jesus Christ views us, and clear about their values and behaviour as a result.

Who are you really? More importantly, whose are you?

I (Marjorie) grew up in Dublin during the 1970s and 80s, the only child of two older parents who were part of the small Anglo-Irish minority. Everything about my life seemed different to those around me. My friends' parents were twenty years younger than mine; our accents were different to everyone else's and for a season I was the only non-Catholic in my school. Catholicism in Ireland defined the people's identity in that era, so being a relatively wealthy 'Proddy' made me stick out like a sore thumb. I remember the day someone wrote on the pavement outside our house 'West-Brits Out' and I innocently asked my dad to whom they were referring. The sign referred to me, and yet I didn't realise it! At that age, I probably didn't really know who I was, but I knew I wasn't a West-Brit. I also knew that I didn't like to feel different, excluded. I wanted to belong, I wanted to be accepted, and I could not work out why that was not always the case.

A confused identity is perhaps nothing new to today's culture or Generations Y and Z. Neither is the longing to belong; to feel part of a tribe, to know whose and who you are.

Wherever you go, there you are

As we disciple the young adults of today, we love their quest for adventure and their big dreaming. Many have entrepreneurial skills and come up with wonderful new creative ideas. We admire how these generations have such a longing to lead a significant life, to be and do something special, and to feel happy as it happens. Yet, when this adventurous spirit is coupled with narcissism or a weak sense of self-identity, the results can be devastating.

The pursuit of happiness can lead to a genuine lack of self-satisfaction or the ability to find peace in the ordinary. Instead, it creates constant movement, uprooting and a lack of commitment to the routines of building a life and an identity steadily in the present. Often, it is not until people we know reach their late twenties and beyond that they tell me they have discovered that one cannot run from oneself, and new places or experiences do not necessarily lead to a new sense of identity.

In other words, you cannot escape yourself: where you go, there you will be. The question is: will you allow God to do the 'interior' work at this point which will create a solid foundation on which to stand for the rest of life?

Know thyself

In our twenty-five years experience of leadership within church, we have come to the conclusion that knowing your identity is the most fundamental question for any young adult. We have also learned not to be afraid of some of the messiness and deconstruction of life and faith that almost inevitably begins as the Holy Spirit is allowed to embark upon His process in someone's life. Our ultimate aim is to guide young people to realise that Christianity lays out an invitation to think and live out of the reality that we are much-loved adopted daughters and sons of a good heavenly Father. And in the process to die to oneself in order to gain the prize of life 'with Christ in God' (Col. 3:3).

The development of a secure identity does not happen overnight. It is the necessary process of what is sometimes called the 'first half of life,' a season which may last into a person's thirties to forties. It cannot be rushed or circumvented.

It is a beautiful stage but it must be attended to because at some point our foundations will be severely tested perhaps by trial, experiencing denial or failure. With solid foundations a person will transition towards the maturity of their 'second half of life'. During our twenties and thirties, the formation of our identity and our sense of security can be significantly distorted if somebody is not equipped or willing to learn from their mistakes, to choose to bounce back during setbacks. This is a time when positive role models and mentors are so vital. However, in our experience, while moving through these stages of life is common to all of us, we have seen that people may become grounded in their sense of identity in Christ at any age. In other words, you can be old in years and still have a fragile identity and you can equally be young in years and live as a child of God.

Space to look below the surface

Apprehending and appropriating our truest identity as children of God is absolutely foundational to receiving Jesus' promise that each of us may experience 'life in all its fullness' (John 10:10, GNT). But focusing on this spiritual truth without digging towards a necessary and complementary emotional maturity and growth can be dangerous for many young adults. Too many spiritual highs, such as vibrant worship scenes or passionate, emotive preaches, can actually destabilise people if not accompanied by an environment in which they are helped to grow in spiritual maturity through one-on-one discipleship. We need spaces in which to challenge and build up a sense of identity not just in the spirit, but in well-formed character and inner resilience. A person's identity that is not rooted in humility and acknowledging our sin and need for God's grace can easily feed a young adult's sense of entitlement and false notion of being more 'special' to those around them. Equally, a young person who engages strongly in a spiritually upward dimension to life, such as in prayer and worship, without the necessary equilibrium of learning to relate well to others and finding God in the messiness of genuine community will soon manifest emotional imbalance in life.

How tragic if we raised emerging adults to be passionate worshippers who had little understanding of their true selves. How dangerous if we raised a generation to know and recite the Scriptures or perform on stages, but who lived crippled with a sense of failure and deep anxiety.

The disease to please affecting Millennials

A recent research report interviewed Christian Millennials who were leaders across a variety of workplace sectors in Britain. Some were confident to say that their identity and security was rooted in being children of God, but instead the majority of responses revealed an underlying tension. Eighty-three per cent said that it was either 'important' or 'very important' to feel liked and validated by those they were leading. A majority also noted 'the need for approval' as the most negative thing affecting their leadership.[44] Naturally humans are performance-driven, competitive, frequently jealous and resentful of each other (just watch an episode of *The Apprentice*). We put huge demands on ourselves, get hurt by others, people-please and compensate for our emotional deficits by unhealthily focusing upon other people. The list goes on.

The danger is that the dominant culture shapes all of us unless we open our eyes and do something about it.

Healthy emotions

In order to mature as an adult, a young person must be given space to understand themselves and to relate well to others. This has been the case since the beginning of time. As John Calvin wisely noted in 1530, 'our wisdom . . . consists almost entirely of two parts: the knowledge of God and ourselves.'[45] Some of the pitfalls of contemporary culture make this process all the more imperative. For example, a lot of young people tell us that although they love the company of their community of friends they frequently feel lonely and can hate to be on their own. They are terrified of creating space, and of what, and who, they might encounter there.

In his book *The Emotionally Healthy Church*,[46] Peter Scazzero emphasises that in order to mature spiritually, one must mature emotionally. The two are intertwined. There are no short cuts to this process. If you engage in spiritual activity but ignore or deny your emotions then you will automatically live with a lack of self-awareness that will have a harmful and damaging effect on yourselves and others.

Jesus was emotional; at times He yelled, raged with anger, wept with grief. In the Garden of Gethsemane He became anxious. He felt and expressed emotion; He was human. In the garden of Gethsemane, He models so powerfully for us the expression of emotion to His heavenly Father that leads Him to a place of total surrender.

As much as Jesus was emotional, He also models for us a life in balance, an integrated life lived from his Father's words of affirmation. He did not allow circumstances to dictate His response. His identity dictated His activity.

The Father's heart

God's heart for the young people around us does not begin with the desire for them to do great things for God and save the planet. It is that they would know how deeply loved they are and allow this truth to foster their faith for the whole of life. No matter how busy life was, no matter all the different swirling desires and opinions of others, no matter His own emotions and desires, Jesus walked out the will of His heavenly Father (John 5:19). Sometimes that meant that He withdrew to the wilderness to spend time with His Dad. At other times, He interacted with the crowds or taught in the busy synagogues.

At the risk of sounding simplistic, we will greatly help the young people around us if we give them permission to express and talk through emotions with us. We will model a good way to live if we teach them to engage with the holy habits such as solitude, Scripture-reading and fasting. In an age where most young people have several electronic devices surrounding them and feeding them with notifications, this is no small challenge. It is a battle worth fighting if we are to help them into acting authentically out of their God-given identity.[47]

Case Study:

The impact of the Father's love for Nick

When I (Nick) was twenty-five I realised that I knew a lot *about* God, but I felt I didn't really *know* God for myself. I entered a season of spiritual pilgrimage and I decided to say 'yes' to God as much as possible. I realised it was time to stop acting like a spiritual orphan, and to start acting like a spiritual son of my heavenly Father.[48] During that time God did the most profound internal business on my heart and head. I came away simply knowing – deep in the root of my soul – that God is my Father and He loves me. Like it had been implanted within me. 'The Father loves me!'

And He is a very good Father.

This is an ever-expanding revelation, and I know there's plenty more to discover – but that truth has become the solid foundation upon which the rest of my Christian life, world view, desires, decisions – even, I suppose, my death – are built upon. It has revolutionised the way I see and live the Christian life. There is just this tremendous sense of security, and a sense of my place and purpose – that I have a part to play in God's plan on earth.

A passion of my life is to pass this revelation on to others. When you know who God is, and who you *are in* God,[49] your life will be revolutionised. Jesus said 'I am the way, the truth, and the life. No one can come to the Father except through me' (John 14:6). Life in all its fulness means knowing our heavenly Father. Security in life is not about a place (heaven), it is about a person (our Father).

Getting the message of evangelism right: 'come home'

Christianity is all about coming home to a very secure place and living within a wonderful family, defined on earth by the truths of heaven. This is the foundation of the Father's love: more significant than working and even suffering for Christ. The problem is that many young adults, even those who have grown up in Christian homes, actually have no idea of their true identity in Christ and the invitation of the secure identity that we have as citizens of a heavenly place (Eph. 2). It is a similar picture beyond the church walls, where there sits a blank canvas of opportunity.

Our church in Sheffield often spends time engaging with everyday people out on the streets. In times of street evangelism over the last few years, we have discovered that this generation is very spiritually hungry. Though they may be totally unchurched and never have stepped into a church service, though the secularisation of schooling has left them often without the most basic knowledge of the Christian faith, a shift has happened in Britain across this generation. They are very interested in a life beyond themselves and the idea of a relationship with God. Time and time again, we hear the same story as we chat to unchurched young people. Often their parents have stepped right away from faith and are atheists or agnostics, but when we raise the possibility of finding a spiritual connection with God, young people will often recall their grandparents' faith, and the resilience and foundations it provided. Suddenly, emerging adults are awakened to explore Christianity as a genuine option. They look at the often broken, dysfunctional lives of their parents and long for a different reality. We have witnessed dozens of young adults come into a healthy church environment for the first time, and come alive in joy, faith and purpose as they experience 'the real thing' – Jesus' definition of 'life in all its fullness' (John 10:10, GNT) – in the family of a local church.

What an opportunity we have as the Church of Britain today to share this message that there is a Father in heaven who deeply loves you.

'Come home!' That is the message we begin with when we share the gospel to the unchurched, and it also resounds with existing Christians. It is a different narrative to the crusades era of Billy Graham two generations ago, which emphasised firstly people as sinner in desperate need of a Saviour. Unchurched people in twenty-first century progressive Western nations tend to be less willing initially to accept that they are sinful or have fallen short.[50] That is why we invite them to 'come home' and have an experience and an encounter with the presence and the love of Jesus. As that occurs, many still fall to their knees recognising their need of His saving grace. At root, it is the same gospel and must be the full gospel of repentance and faith, but re-presented to appeal to the heart and lens of this generation.

A sin crisis or an identity crisis?

At The Well Sheffield when we go onto the streets looking to engage with local people presently far from God, we train our folk to begin simply by approaching people to ask them whether they are aware that there is a Father in heaven who is very interested in them. Everyone we meet on the streets has a sin problem: don't we all! But their sin is not actually the deepest problem, or biggest hurdle. Jesus has already dealt with our problem of sin, if we choose to let Him! The greatest problem is with our sense of identity. A Christian is a person who was once far from God and detached from His family, but is now one with Christ, a union which guarantees that 'every spiritual blessing in the heavenly realms' is ours, 'because we are united with Christ' (Eph. 1:3). We have seen so much deep transformation in the lives of people as the Holy Spirit has revealed this deepest of truths to them. We have met them in our daily lives, at the gym, or the school gate, or among those we have encountered out onthe streets, or who have simply walked through the doors of our church. Many have walked free from addictions instantly and supernaturally; a number look physically different. All of those who have turned to God and received Christ have found a new purpose to life and many are very effectively sharing this new-found life with others.

Their identity was not actually transformed, it was realised. Christians are always the Father's much-loved adopted children: we just do not always realise this truth, or live like it. As identity was discovered, lives were turned upside down. In so doing, people have entered freedom beyond what they had imagined possible. Since the beginning of time, humankind was created in the image of God, placed in the garden with an assignment and authority to rule over the earth and to do so from the place of knowing how deeply loved we are. The message remains 'come home'.

It is easy to love others when you live in a place of security and know how loved you are. Loved people, love people. And deeply changed people have a deeper and longer lasting impact on the world around them, because they are motivated by love.

44. Forge Leadership Consultancy, *Millennial Leaders: Now is Our Time and this is Our Voice* (London: Forge Leadership Consultancy, 2018).
45. John Calvin, trans. Henry Beveridge, The Institutes of the Christian Religion Book I: The Knowledge of God the Creator (London: Bonham Norton, 1599), Chapter 1. Retrieved from Reformed Theology: https://reformed.org/master/index.html?mainframe=/books/institutes/books/indxbk1.html (accessed 5.12.19).
46. Peter Scazzero, The Emotionally Healthy Church (Grand Rapids, MI: Zondervan, 2015).
47. For example, His responses to temptation in the wilderness Matthew 4:1-11.
48. 'I no longer call you slaves . . . Now you are my friends, since I have told you everything the Father told me' John 15:15. (Also John 14:18: 'I will not abandon you as orphans – I will come to you.')
49. We have the right to be called the children of God – see John 1:12.
50. See Romans 3:23.

CHAPTER SEVEN

Fluidity or Freedom According to Jesus?

Identity 2

True freedom means you swap Fathers!

Many Christians do not fully understand, let alone learn to apply what it means to be adopted in Christ. Once we belonged to the 'father of lies' (John 8:44), now all who have become Christians have our home with the 'Father of lights' (James 1:17, NKJV).

> Once you had no identity as a people; now you are God's people. Once you received no mercy; now you have received God's mercy.
>
> *(1 Pet. 2:10)*

As we, the Allans, have taken a personal journey with understanding our sonship, we have a phrase we say to each other as a couple: because of our identity in Christ 'we have nothing to lose and nothing to prove'. This has really meant that we do not so much work *for* God, as *from* God's identity and love in us. It has become about receiving, not achieving. There is a big difference.

Fluidity or freedom?

Our culture emphasises fluidity, but that is not really freedom by Jesus' definition.

Freedom is a very attractive notion to the young in every era. Unfortunately, most live with a counterfeit notion of what true freedom is.

Many young Christians have some understanding of being adopted into the family of God, so that a new identity is bestowed on them. However, we must not miss the important parallels in the Roman adoption process that were at the forefront of the apostle Paul's mind as he wrote these lines:

> you have not received a spirit that makes you fearful slaves. Instead, you received God's Spirit when he adopted you as his own children. Now we call him, 'Abba, Father.' For his Spirit joins with our spirit to affirm that we are God's children. And since we are his children, we are his heirs. In fact, together with Christ we are heirs of God's glory. But if we are to share his glory, we must also share his suffering.
>
> *(Rom. 8:15-17)*

In Paul's era a son of a slave family would frequently have the opportunity to be adopted by a father of the Roman nobility. During an elaborate legal ceremony, there would be an exchange of finance, rather like a ransom or redemption penalty, whereby the new father paid in full for this boy to be taken away from the family and ownership of one man (a slave), and to be adopted into a new family. The boy's whole identity and future changed in an instant. Now the boy was allowed to adopt the new Roman family name and would become an heir to his new father's estate, bearing all the rights and privileges of a son in a noble family of that time.

However, following the Roman adoption process, the slave son wasn't just released to wander off as he pleased, or to set up a new family elsewhere. He passed from the possession of one father to another. The *'Patria Potesta'* of Roman law meant that the living father always retained a power, or ownership, over his son whatever their age. A Christian's truest identity is to be found 'in Christ'. *My* life is not my own, I am now required and empowered to live totally and joyfully submitted to *my* new Father God. That's why Paul elsewhere calls us 'slaves to righteousness.'

> But thanks be to God that, though you used to be slaves to sin, you have come to obey from your heart the pattern of teaching that has now claimed your allegiance. You have been set free from sin and have become slaves to righteousness.
>
> *(Rom. 6:17-18, NIV)*

Identity formation takes time. At Jesus' baptism He heard the words of His heavenly Father 'This is my dearly loved Son, who brings me great joy' (Matt. 3:17). There is no greater voice of approval or affirmation. It takes time for head knowledge to move to heart knowledge and for us to discover that same voice echoes over our lives. We must first help this young generation to understand the incredible invitation on offer, to 'come home', to step into their new identity and then to learn to stay at home: which is the safest, most secure place. Commentators today refer to the Millennial generation as the 'boomerang generation' that does not want to leave home; in the spiritual sense this would be a good thing!

The danger of orphan thinking

Some years ago we volunteered at a children's home in Recife, northern Brazil for a few days. It was home to young boys who had been rescued from the streets. The life of a street boy in

Brazil is very dangerous and precarious. Tragically, these boys had often been abused and had naturally learned to live their life on the defensive. We will never forget the mealtimes as the food was placed on the table. The boys rushed at the table as if it was their last meal, grabbing and hoarding the food, even though there was another meal promised later that day.

Orphans have no sense of security. Orphans carry deep wounds. Orphans live with a sense of lack. Orphans know they need to protect themselves and fend for themselves. Often without realising it Christians may act like spiritual orphans in our thought and actions until we know how deeply loved we are by our heavenly Father.

Personally, we will forever be indebted to those across the body of Christ who have taught and brought revelation on the Father's love for His children and what it means to be adopted as sons and daughters. To walk not as a spiritual orphan but in sonship as one's identity (Gal. 4). This teaching has changed our lives and has given us a tremendous foundation from which to withstand life's storms, and to love and forgive others.[51] For many years now we have made this foundation central to our discipleship of others.

Orphans to heirs

We have found it essential to our lives and leadership to come back and take a stark look at our behaviour, deep thoughts and emotions and examine whether we are feeling and operating more like orphans or sons. Several times a year we will review in our minds the classic symptoms of spiritual orphan-behaviour and ask ourselves some honest questions. Invariably, a particular life challenge or person may have pushed some orphan triggers in us, causing us to act like we have something to prove, or lose. Like we must win or be 'right' or justify ourselves. It is vital that we recognise this and renew our thinking. Sometimes it will be deep wounds of the past such as abandonment that surface and cause undue emotional reactions in us. In other cases, judgement towards others has slipped in. What helps us to release judgement and forgiveness is when we reconnect with who we are in Christ and we allow His grace to flow through us.

Kintsugi – the broken made beautiful

Being Irish, Marjorie loves pottery. We were given much beautiful Irish terracotta pottery as wedding presents, which beautifully clutter up our house. Since we married in 2002, we are always saddened whenever a piece breaks. Each one holds precious memories for us. The pieces simply get swept up, popped in the bin and that's that. There is another way. The Japanese have an art-form called Kintsugi which places a very different value on pottery. We find very inspiring. When their pottery breaks, they glue it back together with golden glue. Rather than being an embarrassment or a failure, the cracks are clearly visible and are considered to make the pottery more beautiful. The most priceless pieces are those that were broken and have been lovingly repaired at the hands of a master. This is such a helpful reminder that we all have areas of brokenness in our lives but if allow ourselves to be reformed by our heavenly Father, the master potter, then He can make broken lives beautiful again.

It is one thing to have an encounter with the Father's love or come to an understanding of His love. It is quite another to mature in your sonship and really live out of that identity.

Identity is first realised and then formed within us as we journey through life and learn to apply biblical truths in the everyday. It is through this forming that we are transformed. In His great grace, God is very good at working all things 'for the good of those who love [Him]' according to His good purposes (Rom. 8:28). We can know the truth of our identity and it will set us free, but only if we learn to believe it and apply it to our lives. Sometimes it is very hard to live only for the Father's embrace and voice, but as life allows us opportunities to do so, we must embrace them, as it is in those places and at those times that we mature in our identity.

Living out the kingdom life 'from' our identity, rather than doing a whole load of stuff 'for' God is a powerful message for today's generations. Jesus was capable of choice and even disobedience but chose only to do what He saw His Father doing (John 5:19) because He first knew just how beloved He was of His Father. That is where our truest empowerment can come from. Of course, 'doing' stuff is very important too. We are created for purpose and work, and the absence of work leaves someone helpless, bored and sometimes depressed. But 'doing' must always flow first from 'being.'

Case Study:

Latifah (age twenty-six)

I know a lot of things about a lot of things. But just knowing something doesn't mean a thing if you don't let that knowledge inform and change you. Otherwise it's just a nice fact. Just a thing that you happen to know. While what you know may remain true regardless of what you do with it, if you don't choose to live like what you know is true, you won't see the fullness. Knowledge without application is powerless. In terms of my identity, this has been one the most important revelations that God, by His grace, has given to me.

I've spent the majority of my twenty-six years on this planet desperately trying to figure out who I am, unknowingly gathering up some incorrect conclusions along the way. Not to say that they were all negative, but still incorrect, nonetheless. I was born during the apartheid in Durban, South Africa so from the start I was thrown into a world that was broken, hurt and divided by the question of identity, and a very shallow view of identity at that. Which side are you on, black or white? As far back as I can remember, I was always uncomfortable and untrusting of who I was. I used to look at myself and think, 'My mum is white, my dad is black, I am neither.' There was a real lack of understanding about who I was. Without God in the picture, the only place I could gather my identity from was the world. If someone were to ask, 'Who are you?' my answer would be made up of elements of my life which I felt defined me. Things like friends, grades, my job, my reputation, my humour, how fast I could down a pint, the fact that I wear odd socks and how long it's taken me to grow my hair. Really all incredibly fleeting and trivial things.

When I first heard about Jesus I really wasn't interested, I think because he seemed like a wet blanket to the fire that was my identity. I loved that I was known for being irresponsible, reckless and drinking a bit too much. All of that stuff about me, as obviously damaging as it was in hindsight, made up my sense of self-comfort and being known. It was who I was! 'So this God wants me to stop all of this and become someone else? I don't think this is for me.'

Regardless of my resistance to Him, God made Himself known to me and showed me that He wasn't a fun sponge and He calls us to live our lives a certain way because He loves us, among many other things. So I came to a place of surrender when I was eighteen. Understanding that He was actually real, I knew I had to respond in some way. I asked for forgiveness and said I was in.

Years later, my journey and relationship with God have gone from strength to strength. Each day I grow to know and love Him more. But I struggled with myself in those years more than ever before. I honestly couldn't understand why

I was finding it so hard to just exist! In hindsight, my identity was utterly broken and founded in the wrong things. I had taken on things that people, the enemy and myself had defined me as, not God. Nonetheless, God continued to meet me where I constantly failed Him and showed me more and more of who He was every step of the way. A God of grace and mercy.

I was part of a ministry school at my church (www.deeper. training) and had taken a year out to commit some time to really pursuing God, in all honesty, quite reluctantly. But God had spoken and He said it was a good idea and I couldn't argue with Him. There was one particular weekend in the year that was dedicated to teaching on identity and God as a Father. It was here that I had the first true revelation about my identity, and it was life-changing. I suddenly understood something that I didn't get before. I knew now that I was a child of God, saved by His grace, made righteous before Him through the sacrifice of Jesus. I knew that I had authority in His name and I was allowed into every room in the King's castle. I'm in the family! I remember thinking, 'It's so simple, how have you not realised this before? We need to get every person in this room right now and tell them all!' It was a powerful gift of revelation for me.

---

51. If you'd like to take this further, we recommend the book *Spiritual Slavery to Spiritual Sonship* by Jack Frost (Shippensburg, PA: Destiny Image, 2013).

CHAPTER EIGHT

Who Am I Not?

Identity 3

I (Marjorie) can remember my shock and sadness the day my loving dad broke the news to me that he thought we should stop paying for ballet lessons because he did not really think I had the physique of a ballet dancer! Years later the same Dad sat me down and advised me against studying law, simply because my character and giftings meant I was poorly suited to an introverted job. Looking back, I'm grateful for the father who loved me so much and believed in me so much that he spoke out truth.

If a first, vital question in young adult disciples is to ask, 'Who am I really?' then it is equally important to be asking an alternative question: 'Who am I not?'

Our society prizes excellence and achievement alongside bigger, better, faster. It is not always very popular to be talking about our limits and limitations. Yet embracing our weaknesses can be key to our growth in self-awareness and acceptance.

Today's culture raises a generation to believe you can be and do anything. There are no limits, just make your choice. Huge emphasis is placed upon growing a child's self-esteem so that natural barriers might be overcome, self-confidence being seen to be the root to successful achievement. After all, today's younger children are being raised by Generation X who grew up singing rather ridiculous songs like R. Kelly's 1998 'I Believe I Can Fly'.

When I was a young child in school there was the annual sports day and there were three prizes for every race: first, second and third. A generation later I attended the sports day of one of my young children. To my amazement, every child who participated in and completed the races got a prize. 'Well done for turning up!' was the attitude. 'Trophies for everyone.'

Trophies for everyone! Be kind and break the news to me . . .

The problem inevitably comes when those children then grow up to discover that in the world of work, sports or academia, there are very real limits. If an emerging adult has not been raised to cope with these harsh truths then their reaction may play out in two ways. Either a twenty-something carries a level of disillusionment, disappointment or potential depression about the true state of things and their lowly place in the pecking order. Or, they have a false sense of self-belief and a lack of self-awareness and carry on regardless with a sense of entitlement. In communities of young people, we can often spot those who are emotionally immature by their total lack of awareness in how they fit with and relate to the crowd. This can often lead to selfish behaviour and a difficulty in establishing deep friendships.

It is a deceptive culture that suggests you can do and be anyone, and which leaves the young confused or sometimes crippled by the apparent limits on their opportunities. Let us not be afraid to offer wise counsel and clear direction towards the grace of God. In His eyes they are spiritual royalty (1 Pet. 2:9) and they are spiritual servants (Rom. 1:1) – a safe place from which to embrace your limits.

I am a child of God, not God Himself

The apostle Paul is perhaps our greatest example in the New Testament of a disciple who walked with authority and anointing, and yet it is fascinating that when questioned by the people in Corinth as to his authority and works, he choose to emphasise not his power, but his weaknesses. He was a child of God, but not God Himself! This is a lesson which all young adults must learn, sooner rather than later.

> And my message and my preaching were very plain. Rather than using clever and persuasive speeches, I relied only on the power of the Holy Spirit.
>
> *(1 Cor. 2:4)*

We would be wise to imitate Paul as he imitated Christ; this is our Christ who considered himself nothing, living a life fully aware of His need of His Father God.[52] Paul boasts in his weakness[53] because he allows them to push him towards a dependency on His heavenly Father. That is where God's power is made manifest.

All discipleship begins with dethroning ourselves, removing ourselves from the centre of the universe and making the risen Christ our Lord. Perhaps we will serve the next generation best if we are careful to present the gospel of being 'hidden with Christ in God' (Col. 3:3). I am wrapped up into His life, not the other way around. His desires become mine, not the other way around.

Churches present a Christianity from the stage that says, 'Invite Jesus into your life.' What if the opposite was true? That He invites you into His life? Getting the starting point right might be very helpful.

We all have limits physically, emotionally, spiritually. When Satan came to tempt humankind in the Garden of Eden the invitation was to eat from the forbidden tree and know all things.[54] In other words, to *be* God. Probably on account of the fact that our culture is not very permission-giving when it comes to weakness, we often want to bypass, hide and work against our weaknesses, not embrace them. A sense of identity that is securely rooted in Christ does not mean that we wipe out weaknesses; instead, we may embrace them.

Knowing the seasons

These truths are vital to explore as we journey with individuals. We live in a culture that puts huge demands on individuals having it all: family, career, further education etc. Many of us operate in church cultures that equally put huge expectations on individuals; it would be natural to feel that one was failing somewhat.

Some of our limits may be seasonal due to stages or circumstances of life. For example, we could be single, or married, or caught up raising children, or battling sickness, or looking after ageing parents. Knowing who we are and knowing and accepting the seasons we find ourselves in can always yield great kingdom fruitfulness whatever the circumstances. Rather than fighting our circumstances and longing for change, we can accept some of the inevitable weaknesses which they produce. We can embrace our limitations. Our weaknesses and limitations (not to be confused with our sin) allow for more of God's identity to be made manifest in and through us.[55] It is the strength of Christ's identity in us (or put more correctly, our identity 'in Him') which gives us the power and potential to overcome, rather than do away with, our weakness and natural limitations.[56]

Limitations

We are not God, nor are we all the same. This means we have limitations on our capacity, understanding, personality. We cannot be anything we choose to be, despite the offers all around us. A life spent copying others is futile. In Romans 12:4-6,

Paul outlines the different giftings given to believers in the body of Christ:

> Just as our bodies have many parts and each part has a special function, so it is with Christ's body. We are many parts of one body, and we all belong to each other. In his grace, God has given us different gifts for doing certain things well.

We have come to realise that a greater sense and transparency as to one's own weaknesses allows for a greater tolerance of weakness in others and equally an ability to really celebrate the differences and gifts of others around us. There is no greater test to sonship than being able to celebrate someone like you being better than you! Failure to train people in this raises a generation dogged with jealousy, comparison and robbed of the peace and joy in who they are.

Getting it the right way around: I have limits but my God is limitless!

If we are sold a limitless vision of ourselves by culture's shaping of us, the same culture does a very good job of putting impressive limits on who God is and what He is capable of doing. This runs the risk of greatly eroding faith in a supernatural, miracle-making God.

It is very important that we don't confuse our identity with that of His.

When it comes to identity, John the Baptist had it nailed. This is how he is introduced as the beginning of John's Gospel:

> Now this was John's testimony when the Jewish leaders in Jerusalem sent priests and Levites to ask him who he was. ... Finally they said, 'Who are you? Give us an answer to take back to those who sent us. What do you say about

yourself?' John replied in the words of Isaiah the prophet, 'I am the voice of one calling in the wilderness, 'Make straight the way for the Lord.'

(John 1:19,22-23, NIV)

John the Baptist was able to root his identity in what the Scriptures said about himself, articulated by Isaiah the prophet and he was equally comfortable pointing the attention away from himself onto the coming Christ. The Scriptures are very clear as to our identity. Just read Ephesians 2 and we discover who we are:

And God raised us up with Christ and seated us with him in the heavenly realms in Christ Jesus, in order that in the coming ages he might show the incomparable riches of his grace, expressed in his kindness to us in Christ Jesus.

(Eph. 2:6-7, NIV)

One of our greatest passions in life is to teach young people and raise a generation confident in this very truth, in who they are in God. But like John the Baptist, who we are finds its expression when held in tension with who we are not. It must have been hard for John the Baptist to see some of his disciples leave him the moment that they realised that Jesus was the new ministry star. However, John seemed not only OK with it, but encouraged it. He knew his role and his place.

The next day John was there again with two of his disciples. When he saw Jesus passing by, he said, 'Look, the Lamb of God!' When the two disciples heard him say this, they followed Jesus.

(John 1:35-37, NIV)

We can only conclude that true significance is found as we embrace who we, and to whom we belong. This is a path to inner peace. It is good to ask ourselves and those we are investing in about the seasons and limitations we have. We may run from our limitations until we realise they are the very doors to humility, direction, communion and revelation.

Case Study:

Nathan (age twenty-six)

As a pharmacist who recently started working in one of the more deprived areas of my city, I have had a stark realisation of the anxiety, depression and mental fragility within the general public, especially among Millennials.

Let me be the first to distinguish the differences between the terms 'mental illness' and 'mental health', both of which are so easily thrown around and misdiagnosed.

Mental health is your state of mental well-being due to circumstances and external factors. Everyone has mental health, it is a spectrum, and we will fluctuate up and down the spectrum as life goes on. In every person's life they will go through seasons of poorer mental health and seasons of stronger mental health. This may manifest in times of peace and joy, and times of despair, anxiety and depression.

Mental illnesses are the change of behaviour, emotions and interactions, usually due to chemical imbalances in the brain. Schizophrenia and chronic depression are examples of mental illnesses. It is possible to have poor mental health and no mental illness, while it is possible to have good mental health with a mental illness.

While mental health can be complex, one thing is for sure: God wants us to think with a heavenly perspective. To bring every thought before him. To think like He would. To grow and help others with problems we have overcome.

On account of my personal and professional experiences, I am passionate about people coming to understand what it means to be a child of God.

My passion for mental health comes from the trials I have been through with it, and the poor mental health epidemic facing Millennials (if you don't believe me, just Google the figures for antidepressant prescriptions broken into age brackets). We as Christians should not shy away from these topics and should face the challenges head-on. For we know that Jesus came to set us free, and this can include freedom from anxiety and depression. While we have compassion, let us disciple people and walk with them through anxiety. And more importantly, let's walk with people and point them in the direction of Jesus, our rock that we are to build our lives upon.

My own journey with mental health starts a few years ago. Having grown up in a middle-class family and gone straight from school into university, I came out and fell victim to the realities that so many Millennials stumble upon: the world doesn't revolve around me. I'm not that special. I can't be anything I want to be. Life consists of many mundane moments.

These truths hit me hard and I crashed and burned after finishing university. Following a break-up with a long-term girlfriend and having to move back in with my parents, I was struck with the situation I was in. I was struck by the foundations that I built my life upon, and how readily it had crumbled beneath me, leaving me with a hopeless despair with a hefty dose of anxiety.

I found myself in the same situation as many other friends my age, which brought some comfort. Single, in a nine to five job and living with my parents, I wondered what my life was about. I wondered how I, the special one, the one that had been told I could achieve anything if I worked hard, that had been told I was qualified to save the world, found myself in this position. Why weren't things working out for the special one?

Little did I realise that God was starting me on the long path to maturity. I had put it off for four wild years of 'education' to come out with a Master's Degree, an ability to drink a pint in under ten seconds and a shattered life.

God had given me the choice to carry on down the empty, barren path I was on, or to return to His abundant way of life. I chose His path with the expectation that life would have meaning and purpose and joy again, which it did, but often God's plan looked nothing like I thought or planned.

I do believe the path to maturity is an everlasting one that we face until we reach heaven, but this becomes easier once we have aligned our values with God's. Once we have fully accepted in every part of our lives, that our lives are not our own, that we have to put aside our desires and give precedence to our King's desires. We have to relinquish being in control.

I am still on the path to maturity and losing my life in the hope that I will find it in Jesus. I am very much still on the path of battling the anxiety that I face. At first I blamed God and swore He was the God of wrath, bestowing punishment upon me for my years of rebellion. I have recently had the revelation that God is good, and actually wants the best for me. A ground-breaking discovery, I know. God is slowly showing me that growing in spiritual maturity can mean decreasing my anxiety. If my identity is fully in God, if I truly believe that I am accepted and have nothing to prove, then why would I be anxious of others' opinions of me, or fear for my job security? If I truly believed that God outrageously loved me, then why would I be anxious at all?

These are the truths I have decided to base my life around. I am still figuring them out and asking God to engrain them into the deepest depths of my subconscious.

Although the past few years have been hard, the path of maturity and overcoming has been one that I know I will look back on and be glad God took me through. Many people never mature and are still self-conscious in old age and live ruled by fear, rather than in the wholeness that God desires for us.

A note on sexual identity: Knowing that you are loved or proving that you are lovable

The 1960s saw the sexual revolution as men and women caught the invitation to sexual freedom and the Church of the time became defensive. Decades later, history repeats and it is so important that the Church of today rises up with a compelling picture of the biblical narrative of both identity and relationship.

Our actions are intrinsically linked to what we believe about ourselves. There is a battle in every human soul to come to terms with a new identity that we all inherit when we become friends and followers of Jesus. The New Testament calls it a 'new nature':

This means that anyone who belongs to Christ has become a new person. The old life is gone; a new life has begun!

(2 Cor. 5:17)

As we have pastored young people over the years, we have noticed that there is a core truth from which each one lives. Simply: they either come to live their lives knowing their secure identity as deeply loved royal sons and daughters of the King;

or, they live their lives with a deep longing to be loved and which can spill over into trying to prove themselves 'lovable' in other people's eyes. For example, we often encounter this when we pastor young women who have been leading sexually promiscuous lives or have had multiple sexual relations outside of marriage, even though their own values tell them to behave differently. There will always be two competing voices when it comes to our identity: the voice of our heavenly Father, and the other which niggles and says 'Did God really say . . .?'[57] At the root of this behaviour is usually a deep desire for affirmation and to feel loved. Sadly, young adults frequently compensate for this deficiency.

Don't make our sexuality everything

We live in a society of deep sexual and spiritual confusion. In 2018 a YouGov survey in the UK found 49 per cent of young adults surveyed would not describe themselves as exclusively heterosexual, instead feeling 'not sure' of their sexual gender.[58] This points to a lot of anxiety and a lot of confusion. The same year The Daily Telegraph newspaper wrote on sexual fluidity, advocating that society should no longer use binary labels for sexuality – such as heterosexual or homosexual – because people should now be free to follow their desires moment by moment.[59]

At the heart of this confusion lies a contemporary train of thought that effectively argues we 'are' our desires. That our desires drive and derive our identity. For example, I have same-sex attraction, I am affirmed in my desire, therefore that becomes 'who I am'. 'I am gay, I am bi, I am straight' and so on. Taken to its conclusion, this means that the group whom a person identifies with becomes their whole identity, right at the core of who you believe they are.

All of a sudden, an orientation or a desire has been given a massive power and allowed to define the root of our identity. Jenell

Williams Paris, an anthropologist at the University of Pennsylvania describes this in her book *The End of Sexual Identity*.[60] She opens the book with this: 'Sexual desire is now considered central to human identity and sexual self-expression is seen to be essential by many for healthy wellbeing. This is new.'

We are allowing the truest thing about us to be defined as our sexual attraction and desire. People are placing their sexuality as higher in the pecking order than their faith, or their family, or their livelihoods in explaining their identity. It should never become the case that the truest thing about me is who I want to have sex with.

Of course, sexuality is a complex and personal matter and must be handled with great care and extreme love. But it was never instituted by God to become what defines our whole identity. Parts of the Western Church are in danger of being shaped more by society than by biblical values. Unless we step back and help others first engage with their identity in its deepest, truest sense as adored children in union with God, then our conversations will become increasingly confused, complex and controversial.

It is really important that we do not come up with answers or impose our views. But rather, we learn to come alongside people and journey with them as they discover God.

---

52. For example, see 1 Corinthians 11:1; Philippians 2:5-8.
53. 2 Corinthians 12:9.
54. Genesis 3.
55. 2 Corinthians 12:9.
56. Ephesians 6:13.
57. Genesis 3:1.
58. 2018 YouGov, https://yougov.co.uk/topics/relationships/articles-reports/2019/07/03/one-five-young-people-identify-gay-lesbian-or-bise (accessed 6.12.19).
59. Rebecca Reid, 'No One Is 100pc Straight and the Sooner More Men Embrace That the Better', *The Telegraph*, Telegraph Media Group, 15 March 2018, www.telegraph.co.uk/women/sex/no-one-100-straight-sooner-men-embrace-better/ (accessed 6.12.19).
60. Jenell Williams Paris, *The End of Sexual Identity: Why Sex is Too Important to Define Who We Are* (Downers Grove, IL: IVP, 2011).

CHAPTER NINE

A Perfect Flat White in a Lonely Café Corner

The greatest disease in the West today is not TB or leprosy; it is being unwanted, unloved, and uncared for. We can cure physical diseases with medicine, but the only cure for loneliness, despair, and hopelessness is love. There are many in the world who are dying for a piece of bread but there are many more dying for a little love. The poverty in the West is a different kind of poverty – it is not only a poverty of loneliness but also of spirituality. There's a hunger for love, as there is a hunger for God.

(Mother Teresa)[61]

In early 2018 then British Prime Minister Theresa May took an unusual move when she appointed a Minister for Loneliness. 'For far too many people loneliness is the sad reality of modern life', said Mrs May. 'I want to confront this challenge for our society and for all of us to take action to address the loneliness endured by the elderly, by carers, by those who have lost loved ones – people who have no one to talk to, to share their thoughts and experiences with.'[62]

In fact, isolation or loneliness runs wider in our society than Mrs May suggests. The younger generations may apparently be connected to hundreds of people and may have 24/7 contact with others in this digital age and yet be the loneliest generation to date. More than 9 million people in the country often or always feel lonely, according to a 2017 report published by the Jo Cox Commission on Loneliness. As Jo Cox said, 'Young or old, loneliness doesn't discriminate.'[63]

Connected but not in community

A young woman in our church surprised me recently when she told me the story of one of her female friends in her twenties being chatted up in a bar one night. Frustrated by this young man's approaches, the girl exclaimed, 'What are you doing? If I wanted to be picked up by somebody I would be at home in my pyjamas on my phone! Instead I'm out for the night with my girlfriends and I have no desire to meet any man.' This story highlights some of today's changes within social relationships. In previous times we went out for the night to meet a potential partner. In today's culture many connections happen at home through online dating apps like Tinder or SALT.

Many university students today report that they stay locked in their rooms for days on end because they feel rejected or that they don't really fit in. Very quickly loneliness can turn into depression. Doctors we know in our own city anecdotally report that bad mental health among students is increasing at an alarming rate. Many secondary school children express feelings of isolation despite being the most digitally connected generation ever, and society is full of concerns for teenagers' mental health. Many young adults, being that bit older, can recognise that they often have issues around social anxiety in group settings because of the lack of contexts in which they have meaningful relationships.

This is because connection and community are two totally different realities. You can be connected to hundreds of people and still have no meaningful relationships. One person can feel lonely in the company of others, while another can feel truly and deeply connected when in solitude.

Individual or community life?

Remarkably, many young people today report that they have no meaningful social support at all — not a single person they can confide in. Many report having no close confidants or friends outside their immediate family. For some, close family is not even an option because in their past they have experienced disruptions like parental break-ups, which leaves some feeling as if they have no one to turn to. Our culture is experiencing an epidemic of loneliness.

In our hyper-connected world, how could this happen?

It is the result of hundreds of little things. You can probably think of several off the top of your head: the long commute or remote working, the lure of the internet, personal phones which mean you don't even raise your head in public anymore . . .

Today's culture is the most information connected, yet the least relationally connected ever to be formed. Only fifty years ago in Britain we benefited from a richness of community life that has virtually disappeared. It has supposedly become virtual, but it has, in fact, become a thing of the past. In any urban context we have been witnesses to a long, slow retreat into the sealed comfort of our fortress-like homes. Deep friendships formed by regular casual social interaction over the garden fence or in the local pub/club have been replaced by screens, gadgets and exhausted couch-potato stupor. Perhaps the COVID-19 pandemic of 2020 will have a lasting impact of reversing these trends, as local communities connected in new ways to pull-together in a time of crisis.

We were never designed to live like this. For the great majority of human history, people resided in small, intimate communities with shared purpose. Anthropologists who spend time with modern-day settled agrarian nations report that social isolation and loneliness are largely unknown among them: group members spend the bulk of their time – virtually all day, every day – in the company of friends and loved ones. Since the Industrial Revolution, people have been forced into ever-closer proximity to live and work alongside each other. The digital age is starting to unravel this. In today's urban culture it is possible to spend an entire day surrounded by people – and speak to nobody. We have all witnessed young adults drinking their perfect flat white coffee in a café beautifully designed to enhance community, yet they've chosen to speak to nobody else present, perhaps not even to make eye contact.

What can we do?

It is a real step forward that the UK government has acknowledged and wants to tackle this large and growing problem of loneliness. Working out what to do about the problem is harder. As Christians we have a very real understanding that only God can change a person from the inside out. And we have a secret weapon in the war on loneliness, often hidden in plain sight: the average church congregation!

As the newspaper journalist Deborah Orr observes:

> The great prophylactic against loneliness is feeling that you are part of something bigger than yourself – a family, a friendship group, a community, a benign universe, whatever. Even a community with little in the way of material resources finds some contentment in being in a group of people who are all in it together.[64]

This is where the Church has such an opportunity! We are part of something beyond ourselves. It is not an organisation, it is an organism, a movement, circulating the planet over the last 2,000 years. Movement means it is alive and it changes lives. Movements attract people. The worldwide Church is a community of people with a cause beyond themselves. And it is permanently open to newcomers.

Within any average local church community there are tremendously powerful connections. Connections more real than our contemporary digital culture could ever dream of. True conversion to Christ means you have one faith and are baptised into the one family, as the apostle Paul writes in the New Testament.[65] But it still requires effort on our part to help this strength of connection to be felt by new joiners.

Locating yourself in the big story

The first task of evangelism is to help connect the dots for people with how Christ responds to them individually and their story. The second task is about broadening their horizons, temporal and eternal, as we help them know where they fit within the big story, and the big family of God. The same principles apply in discipling young adults. Where does our story fit within the God story? To discover this helps us greatly in our quest for self-fulfilment.

From creation to revelation, God is writing the story of a Father in heaven who loves us and who is drawing us home to be in relationship with Him. From the beginning to the end of time the DNA of His kingdom contains resurrection power. He proclaims: 'Look, I am making everything new!' (Rev. 21:5). He is massively into redemption. We Christians are not waiting smugly to go to heaven when we die, we are caught up in a tremendously broad and exciting cause: 'making everything new' around us. We are characters in the most exciting story ever told, and as we come into relationship with Christ we get to write the next chapters.

The Cox Commission report mentions social institutions that are becoming a less and less common aspect of people's daily lives – church, local pub, workplace, social club. Schools feel like high-pressure environments rather than places where people are nurtured and led through childhood. Even corner shops have changed beyond recognition.

Again, what an opportunity we have! It is no wonder that as new church plants spring up in old buildings across city centres of urban Britain, they are often full within a few weeks of opening. There is a longing to be part of something, something vibrant and alive. Part of a community which communicates: 'You can be part of us and part of something bigger.'

The young and old make the best of friends – Jonny's story

Tragically, a few years ago we attended the funeral of a young adult man, Jonny, who we had known and led in a former congregation. This wonderful lad who appeared to have all of life before him died very suddenly in a car crash aged twenty-two. This tragedy rocked the world of the young adult community around him. This wonderfully vibrant, popular character appeared on someone's social media feed most days of the week. He was the party king who changed atmospheres with his big smile. Yet as his church ministers, we were very aware that Jonny, like many of his peers, had his fair share of brokenness. But something was revealed at his memorial service that really caught our attention. Even though Jonny had been part of a large vibrant young adult community and had attended our discipleship school, he had done a lot of his processing about life with an older lady. We knew many of Jonny's best mates, but it was a surprise when Annie got up to speak about Jonny's life.

it soon became apparent that Annie had known him, really known him, more than most of us. Annie had been Jonny's youth leader at his home church. Coming from an unchurched family he had spent much time in her home. During that funeral service she told a number of wonderful stories of how together they had circled her garden chatting deeply on many occasions. She showed a photo of her garden bench where they had sat working out life. It would now be known with sadness and deep fondness as 'Jonny's bench'.

Older Annie never appeared in his Facebook photos, but she was clearly instrumental in Jonny's walk as a disciple of Jesus. She was his safe space.

'Jonny was one of those young lads who was all-or-nothing,' Annie later told us. 'He could blow hot or cold, depending upon the day. But over time I witnessed the Labrador puppy grow into a strong dog.' Most significantly, she emphasised, 'I learned so much from Jonny. I learned as much from him about life as he did from me.' Discipleship is always two-way.

So, whoever you are, whatever stage of life or life experience, know that you can have a significant role in the shaping of the younger generations. It is never about being trendy. Annie was available. She was kind. She listened and she probably had a great deal of wisdom. Little did she know that in her older age, she was preparing a young man to meet His Maker.

---

61. Mother Teresa (compiled by Lucinda Vardey), *A Simple Path* (New York: Ballantine Books, 1995).
62. 'PM Commits to Government-Wide Drive to Tackle Loneliness', *GOV.UK*, UK Government, 17 January 2018, www.gov.uk/government/news/pm-commits-to-government-wide-drive-to-tackle-loneliness (accessed 6.12.18).
63. Dan Howard, 'Newspaper Column: Simple Steps to Tackling Loneliness and Isolation', *Jo Cox MP*, 15 December 2015, www.jocox.org.uk/2015/12/11/newspaper-column-simple-steps-to-tackling-loneliness-and-isolation/ (accessed 6.12.19).
64. Deborah Orr, 'Modern Life Is Lonely. We All Need Someone to Help', *The Guardian*, ©Guardian News and Media Ltd, 16 December 2017, www.theguardian.com/commentisfree/2017/dec/16/modern-life-lonely-isolation-hardwired-lives (accessed 6.12.19).
65. Ephesians 4:5-6.

CHAPTER TEN

Authentic Community

Most churches today do not just operate as one single gathering of people. They have multiple groups within them: small groups, life groups, home groups, missional communities, call them what you will. When we use the word 'community' in the context of church, what do we mean? It is a small-to-mid-sized group of people who commit to share aspects of life and Christian journey together, and who allow themselves to know one another, and be known.

When forming a new community at The Well Sheffield we ask all our community leaders to form their rhythm around the practice of the early Church in Acts 2:

- They meet together in homes

- They eat together when they meet

- They read the Scripture together

- They pray together

- There is an expectation for signs, wonders and miracles

- They share resources (sometimes simply the home and food)

- They have a cause beyond themselves — whether that is reaching out to others, serving the city together, or simply being open to welcome in new people

This is typical in many churches, but not in most non-Christians' lives.

Community life requires us to give of our time, our tables, our pockets. People's lives can be broken and require our time, our attention and compassion. Yet it is through sharing our personal lives that the kingdom life often flows most powerfully.

Recently, we spoke to some unchurched people who had come to visit our church. They had never previously been interested coming to church, but they had attended a thanksgiving meal in one of our communities and were very struck by the love between the people who came from different nations and had very different social backgrounds. They had never experienced anything like it and found it hugely attractive.

Don't confuse community with chemistry

There is a big difference between friendship and authentic community.

In my Christian or professional life, I (Marjorie) have connected with many national leaders we have come to know over the years and also met some wonderful new friends. While I will hope to be polite to everyone, I will also have my favourites! The ones I love to grab a coffee with, the ones who think like me, the ones who have a similar spirituality. Some of these natural connections have developed to become close friends. We like each other because we are like each other! There's a natural chemistry – it is easy to relate. My friend Chlo is someone like this in my life. She is also the joint senior leader of a church, with her husband. I love the way she prays. Her walk with God always inspires me. I always love our chats and I'd like to wear the clothes she wears!

Chlo is my friend but she is not in my community. She lives in London and I see her twice a year for a few days only. We do not do life together. My friend Amanda, on the other hand, sees me most days of the week. We do life together. Our children go to the same schools. We go to the same church. We are in the same community group. We do ministry together. Amanda sees me on good days and we celebrate life together. We have seen some of the same people healed and saved, and we share the same kingdom triumphs. We go to parties together, holidays, nights out, and our families celebrate Christmas together. Amanda sees me on my bad days and she is kind to me. When I am anxious, she can tell. When I had a potentially bad report in the hospital, it was Amanda who I phoned from the car park. If I need to process life, I go round for a cup of tea. She speaks truth and challenges me. I may be her church leader, but I am not above her. When I experience grief and pressure, she is there for me. A life shared with others can be a life halved of its burdens.

We choose our friends. We do not necessarily choose our community. It is a bit more like blood family in that respect. There are people in our community who are not like me. We have a lot of children in our community, they are all very different and they can be 'character forming' for us all! But God has given us those children and I love them and they shape me in return. Church community (doing life together, sharing yourselves, eating together, praying together) has the ability like nothing else to test us, expose us, challenge us and shape us. In fact, it is actually impossible to walk out discipleship on your own. The Trinity are in deep committed relationships with each other and they call us to live the same way.

Many young adults attempt to walk out their faith on their own because of the individualistic nature of life these days. Community is scary; so is submission to leaders who will speak into your life and challenge you. Sometimes it feels easier to stay in your bedroom and listen to podcasts from a church on the other side of the world. There is nothing wrong with listening to podcasts – they are an amazing resource. But a spiritual diet which is so individualistic is rather like eating alone: it will never satisfy or develop and mature you in the way that communal life does.

Our encouragement is to dive into church community – the young, the old, the poor, the rich, all the wonderful messiness of it, because in the process you will discover yourself!

Up close and personal

The first people whom the Allans disciple are, of course, our own Generation Z children. Our challenge is to I allow them to see our Christian life with intentionality. Do I allow them to see my relationship with God, or is this something hidden and private, to which they have no access?

As my teenagers navigate the storms of life, will they have experienced and witnessed first-hand where my anchor holds, enough to imitate me? This is a challenge to Nick because he tends to be a more introverted person and he needs space to recharge from a vocation which is people-focused. But we live in community. Who are the people up close to you? Are they your flatmates, colleagues, siblings? This is an opportunity for discipleship at its best. Sometimes it hurts, sometimes it is inconvenient, but we know it is the better path, not just because of how we can invest into others, but because it is good for our character development too.

Part of a tribe but not tribalism

A shared commitment to a cause such as the church-in-mission gives us a real purpose to life. Commitment to a cause and commitment to each other breeds this tremendous sense of family. The feeling you are part of a tribe. Jesus was continually giving the invitation to be part of His new tribe, but He was not into tribalism.

Tribalism seems to be on the rise in the West. Never before has modern Britain been so divided. The traditional dividing lines of politics and religion have long been eroded and have been replaced by 'issue centred' factions. For example, a young adult recently told us that the first question they asked of a potential partner on a dating website was: 'Are you for Brexit or Remaining in the EU?'

Family was Jesus' most radical idea. He called His disciples His true family: 'these are my mother and brothers', he said (Mark 3:34). Then he called His followers to do the same. And what a blended family it was! Mathew the tax collector worked for the Romans and he found himself part of the same cause as Simon the Zealot, the anti-establishment terrorist. It would be like calling the Islamic State terrorist and the White Supremacist to come together. Jesus was not afraid to do this. He is unity.[66] He is part of a family with the Father and Spirit that draws us into community and reproduces family.[67] He seems to relish eroding differences. The movement He began continued in the same vein. Paul and Silas travelled to Philippi in Acts 16 and established the church there with Lydia the Macedonian businesswoman, the slave girl delivered of a demon (two women on opposite ends of the social spectrum) and the Roman jailer. It grew to be one of the most mature churches in the New Testament.

Tribalism has been described as 'the dark twin of Individualism' in our Western culture today.[68] Isolation breeds self-centredness and division. Jesus' heart beats to a very different rhythm and He is looking for those who will see others with the Father's eyes.

A community that can hold together tensions and differences of opinion is very countercultural today. It becomes very interesting and appealing to the outside world. Like Jesus says, 'Your love for one another will prove to the world that you are my disciples' (John 13:35). In this era of polarised politics and opposing opinions, it is inevitable that Christians at times will come to very different conclusions as to what the kingdom of God looks like in practice. We will all have cultural blind spots.

We, the Allans, spent a little time ministering in America's Bible Belt. It did not take long to notice many culturally specific practices and beliefs which powerfully shape the way people follow God, yet their outlook feels a million miles away from the liberal-minded Brits we are usually around. But we do not have to travel the seas to find our differences. In our own local church communities you will find people on opposites sides of the spectrum: pro/anti-Trump, pro/anti-Brexit . . . the list goes on. The body of Christ does not have to lay aside our differences, but we are commanded to unite around our common cause, to respect others and to listen well.[69] The average church may be emerging as one of the last truly 'safe' spaces where divergent views and relationships can genuinely hold together – because they are held together in God's love.

The challenge of vulnerability

It is no secret that young adults value vulnerability. They see through any intent to cover-up and Generation Z in particular can be very cynical about leaders on a pedestal. Celebrity and political scandals combined with inherent institutional mistrust have compounded this. Just think about the revelations of abuse at the hands of significant people in positions of power across the Church, sports, politics and Hollywood over recent years. It is clear that trust in leadership can only be restored by honest conversation; acknowledgement of weaknesses, accountability and environments where people are free to ask questions and there is not an overexercise of power.

But for all the talk of vulnerability, our observation is that the emerging generations don't necessary 'do' vulnerability very well. They do not necessarily know how to be genuinely and safely vulnerable. On the contrary, traumas such as abuse, family breakdown or mental ill health and anxiety mean that many young adults have numbed their emotions since childhood as a coping mechanism. Such mechanisms can be necessary and successful, but they come at the expense of two common consequences. Firstly, you can only bury emotions for a period of time. While you might successfully hide them for a decade, anger or frustration will inevitably surface. Secondly, if you unconsciously learn to freeze certain emotions, you will inevitably become someone who finds it hard to engage with the full range of your emotions. 'We cannot selectively numb emotions. When we numb the painful emotion, we also numb the positive emotion', said Dr Brené Brown, a University of Houston researcher whose popular work focuses on the need for vulnerability and what happens when we desensitise ourselves to it.[70]

Virtual vulnerability

Aspects of contemporary young adult culture also contribute to bad emotional health. The current dating and relationships scene where you 'hang out' and 'hook up' without entering into any form of committed relationship fuels feelings of insecurity and encourages efforts to hide real feelings. 'Why weren't you honest with him about how you were feeling?' Marjorie recently asked a young woman. As she reflected on the current confusion which surrounded her romantic relationship, she answered, 'I guess I didn't want to appear needy.'

The way young people date can sometimes put them into an emotionally vulnerable position long before their relationship has reached the stage when it can cope. Recently, a Gen Y girl told us how she felt rejected and exposed after using a dating app. It is as simple as one swipe on your phone to begin a virtual relationship with somebody. She began a conversation through an app which quickly morphed beyond pleasantries into the virtual couple sharing a *lot* of information about themselves: likes, dislikes, did they want children, hopes for the future and so on. This continued until they met in the flesh. After that the man showed no interest in taking the relationship forward and never contacted her again. She felt deep heartache at having opened herself up yet getting nothing back.

Those of us in a position to mentor Generations Y and Z should be alert to the potentially unhealthy sides of the contemporary dating scene, and actively help people to avoid such pitfalls by exercising wisdom ahead of time.

Neither are these deep wounds automatically healed at the altar of marriage. The average marriage age for Generation Y is postponed now until twenty-nine for men and at least twenty-seven for women. They may have been dating various people for up to a decade before marriage. That is a lot of time for deep emotional wounds to form. As church leaders, it is increasingly concerning for us how many young adult married couples face huge challenges in the first few years of marriage. They carried their issues into their relationship, hoping the perfect (at least, it looked perfect on Instagram) marriage would medicate their prior addictions, anxieties or prejudices. They quickly learned that it does not take a long time living in close proximity to one's new partner for one's selfishness and brokenness to resurface!

Vulnerability according to the Bible

then I shall know fully, even as I am fully known.

(1 Cor. 13:12, NIV)

Every person is designed for connection. It is our whole purpose in life with each other and God. Connection at any level means we have to allow ourselves to be seen. Vulnerability is absolutely essential for any disciple who wants to walk with integrity, avoid temptations, build healthy relationships and heal the hurts of the past. Christian maturity is partly about growing into the reality that when we walk out our lives as sons and daughters of the King, we can discover the most stable foundation from which it is genuinely safe to be vulnerable.

It is not vulnerability for the sake of it. We can be vulnerable because we have nothing to lose and nothing to prove. We are already deeply loved. Our heavenly Father loves us when it is sunny and when it rains. He loves us when we do well and when we mess up. Nothing we can ever do will change His love for us. And that is why we can be vulnerable with Him, and as a result, vulnerable yet secure with others.

Our life can be about receiving His love, not working to achieve it.

So why do we resist vulnerability?

'In order for connection to happen, we have to allow ourselves to be seen, really seen' comments Brené Brown.[71] Vulnerability is not a modern concept – it actually began back in Eden. Adam and Eve 'were both naked, but they felt no shame' before their Maker (Gen. 2:25). They walked as children of God in the way life was always intended to be. Only when they overstepped the boundaries did they want to hide from Him in shame.

At the Fall, two sentiments surfaced which have the power to control our inner dialogue: fear and shame.

Fear says, 'Something bad may happen to me at any point.'

Shame says, 'There is something wrong with me.'

Fear and shame kill vulnerability.

Fear tells you other people are not safe. 'If people see this about me, they won't love me.' Shame stops you from sharing. 'I'm not good enough, smart enough, beautiful enough.'

Therefore: 'I am not enough.'

There is a powerful alternative, laid out on the pages of the New Testament. It is about walking in sonship, following in the footsteps of Jesus. It is an invitation to live our lives like the picture of Eden, where we are free to be vulnerable. It is possible to live as a secure son and daughter of God because, at the cross, the root causes of fear and shame in our lives were put to death alongside Jesus. Being much-loved sons and daughters means that our feelings no longer need to dominate. We do not need to win an argument, to make the person fancy us, be seen to be successful and so forth, in order to feel good or avoid shame.

THE XYZ OF DESCIPLESHIP

This is true vulnerability, and it is much easier for any follower of Jesus. It is different to the popular understanding of vulnerability. It is both the 'Why' and the 'How' of vulnerability.

The 'controlling' alternative

If we do not walk out our lives with a value on vulnerability, we will inevitably seek to be in control and to over-assert ourselves. This might happen in the form of addictive patterns, exercising control over others' behaviour, thoughts and actions, or seeking to control our environments.

There are lots of symptoms of being influenced by fear or shame. Nobody wants them. Nobody really wants to be that nagging spouse. Or to be in rebellion, or find themselves critical of their church leaders. People like to be in control, but good leaders do not want to control others. No leader wants to control the people they lead, or to hold offence and resentment towards those we serve. Nobody wishes to be crippled by people-pleasing, waking up to check our phones for 'likes', texts, some signs of affirmation.

All of the above are symptoms of fear and shame and the outworking of control. All of them are avoidable as we embrace our true identity as children of God, and allow the power of loving, non-judgemental Christian community to help us to be vulnerable enough to face up to our shortfalls, and journey towards a more Christ-like character.

Intentionally creating space for real, raw relationships

Many young adults recognise their weaknesses. Churches, mentors and peers can have a significant role in creating relationships of trust and environments of love where it is OK not to be OK and where a vision for 'wholeness' and emotional health can be modelled and understood. People who learn to live in vulnerability learn to love themselves and others well.

Living in vulnerability is being real, it means we live aware of our weakness but with a real sense of worthiness that comes from God. It is the most real kind of life – one defined by the freedom to love ourselves and others.[72]

We can grow in vulnerability and help others to do so as we give time to understand ourselves, our areas of fear and shame, our true identity. It allows our shadow sides, our untamed emotions, our past hurts, our less than pure motives that we live largely unconscious of, but which strongly influence our behaviours, to surface in a safe place.

Older leaders and disciplers can have a role, whatever our context, in training and teaching in identity and being vulnerable as we do so. There are things we can also do in church and home life to create a culture and environment which can really help young adults in this journey. If we are to help young adults to walk as disciples, they need to be able to have close enough access to us to imitate our lives, to see us on a regular basis, including our weaknesses and wrestles, not the crafted public version. In turn, this will help young adults to feel safe and willing to open up their lives to the discipleship process.

Case Study:

How Nick was discipled in his twenties

When I (Nick) was aged twenty-four to twenty-eight, I was intentionally discipled by some Sheffield church leaders as I voluntarily served within the local church. I had responded to their invitation to join them in bringing life and transformation to an inner-city church in a deprived area of Sheffield. I think I was aware that when I joined them on mission I would be the real beneficiary. They were radical disciples of Jesus who had moved to engage in cross-cultural mission and I could see their passion and dedication would rub off on me. It did, and I learned so much from them over the next few years. They did not just invite me to help them run church programmes with them, they invited me to share their lives.

This family opened their home and lives to me. I could arrive at the door without invitation. I knew I could help myself to their food. I shared in the chores and knew I needed to be willing to babysit their four boys (always great fun). We talked life as we sorted laundry, we talked theology over cups of tea. I processed my future marriage as we walked the streets doing door-knocking evangelism. I learned to trust their opinions – a lot. There was purpose to our relationship as we engaged together in incarnational mission and in reaching the neighbourhood. Purpose in relationships matters. They were not perfect, they had grumpy days and bad hair days, but I watched them turn consistently to God and each other in times of weakness and pressure. They discipled me life on life. Ever since then, Marjorie and I have opened our home and lives to many young adults in a similar way.

Getting intentional

Many young adults like to share houses together or live with families in our city. But living in the same house is not the same as shared discipleship. This requires intentionality and deliberate depth in conversation.

In my mid-twenties in Sheffield I (Nick) was part of a small 'huddle' discipleship group with several other young men. We ate together, we prayed and fasted together, studied the Bible and discipleship books together, and shared a common cause of outreach and local church mission. We formed a band of brothers for that period of pre-married life.

This was a reflective group largely centred on two questions: 'What is God saying to you?' and 'What will you do about it?' It was a place where the discipler leading it could share from his life and habits and we could respond. It was a place where we could be honest as to what was going on for us. Over time trust was built up, and if I made mistakes in life or had questions, I knew where to go. They loved me, were committed to me and what was best for me, and I knew it. They set the bar high in terms of faith and expectation. If I messed up, I could be honest about it, but they challenged me not to repeat it, but to change instead. They challenged and trained me in the spiritual disciplines, the holy ancient habits which shape us as followers. Together we went on spiritual journeys together, like all praying for the same breakthrough or to speak in tongues,[73] or fasting on the same days. It was fun! It was deep community.

Today we (both Marjorie and Nick) make a point of running many such 'huddle' discipleship groups in our local church. We intentionally draw younger leaders into relationship with us, in same-gender groups, and invite them to process their life and faith. The type and purpose of the group varies. Some of the people are community leaders in the church, others are young men and women with potential, or people that God has simply shown us we should invest in. The questions we generally ask of ourselves have not really changed: 'Who is God, what is He asking of me? Now hold me to account to do something about it.'

Some of these groups happen in the early morning, some in workplaces, others in the evening. Whatever works. We consider it is one of the best investments of our time. And we have both found that for all the talk of vulnerability, it is not any easier for someone to make themselves known today as it was twenty years ago. If we can create a culture and deliberate environments such as these discipleship groups where people are given the time and space to be real and be heard and be invested in, we will raise disciples.

66. John 10:30.
67. Matthew 11:27; John 16:14; 2 Corinthians 13:14.
68. David Brooks in an interview with Colin Hansen published as a transcript of The Gospel Coalition Podcast, 29 April 2019. https://www.thegospelcoalition.org/podcasts/tgc-podcast/david-brooks-journey-wandering-jew-confused-christian/ (accessed 6.12.19).
69. For example, 1 Peter 3:15.
70. Brené Brown, 'The Power of Vulnerability', TED Talk June 2010. To watch the full talk, visit TED.com
71. Ibid. See endnote 70.
72. Psalm 139 is a beautiful example of this way of thinking and living.
73. To read more about the spiritual gifts, see Acts 19:6; 1 Corinthians 14.

CHAPTER ELEVEN

Life Around the Table

Even if your cupboards are bare, offer them
scrambled eggs . . .

Growing up in Dublin in the 1970 and 80s, I (Marjorie) experienced a taste of Ireland in its traditional sense, before it grew wealthier, busier and more cosmopolitan. Hospitality was central to our culture: life revolved around the kitchen table. The sense of local community was very strong. We knew our neighbours, most families attended the church up the road, schooling was local. Nobody had a lot of spare cash, a lot of life was shared. Ireland was all about people. People's news, people's families, people's tragedies and triumphs. In our local neighbourhoods we would continuously 'drop in', visiting each other. People rarely prearranged their visits – they would simply and spontaneously drop in for a chat and a cup of tea. 'Calling in' on people was a sign of your love for them and your interest in them.

Hospitality was, and is to this day, of the highest value for my mother. She is a true Irishwoman! She baked every morning. I can still smell the fresh bread and scones, and I so loved the constant supply of flapjack and fruit cake. It was ready at all times to be offered to any visitor who dropped in. I remember her training me as a young woman with the words, 'Even if your cupboards are bare, offer them scrambled eggs; but always offer food to any person who steps over your threshold.' And so she fed the neighbours, the gas man, mothers from the school, the window cleaner, and in later years my young adult friends from university and church. She stopped her tasks, made an extra space at the table and sat down with them, chatting over endless cups of tea.

We always ate our family meals together around the kitchen table, and it would not be surprising as a child to discover that somebody else would unexpectedly join us. I can remember occasions when a visitor would drop in unexpectedly just after we had served our food onto our plates. Before they made it from the hallway into the kitchen, my mum would whip our plates away and divide up our food among the newly expanded table. It was a wonderfully warm and welcoming home, and my parents' hospitality is remembered by people many years later.

Looking back, I realise that what I experienced and have sought to replicate during my adult life wasn't simply about being Irish. These day-to-day practices were rooted in my parents' deeply held Christian principles forming a rhythm which allowed the kingdom of heaven to break out on earth. Many tears were shed around my mother's table, dreams were conceived, and relationships mended. Stories of the past were retold and faith grew. Big prayers were spontaneously prayed and hope rekindled. New introductions were made and relationships blossomed, lessons were taught and hearts were healed. This fruitful and powerful legacy continues to this day in the same spot, and she still owns the same table.

There is no other context quite like community around a table.

The first church was birthed around a table

The first church was a meal around a table. Jesus ate with His disciples, ate with those closest, ate with sinners and the lost. The most intimate conversations happened around the table, eating together, including Jesus' final instructions to His disciples on what was about to follow.[74]

The early Church was formed as community ate together: 'All the believers devoted themselves to the apostles' teaching, and to fellowship, and to sharing in meals (including the Lord's Supper), and to prayer' (Acts 2:42). The Church at its core was a community around a table. Celebrating communion or the Eucharist which Jesus inaugurated was a community occasion, a love feast. It was never meant to be a staged event where a priest provides a service to religious consumers in pews.

An untabled faith is an unstable faith. A neglect of the table in our churches is echoed in our families and communities.

(Leonard Sweet)[75]

I'm not used to table living

More than one in five families only sit down to eat a meal together once or twice a week, according to one survey. And 40 per cent of families only sit down together to have a meal three times a week. Just over one in five families in the UK take their 'family meals' in the sitting room on the sofa in front of the television.[76] In Britain for so many generations family was the building block of society and eating together was central to what it meant to be 'family'. Yet to today's younger generations, the image of family around a table seems very out of date.

In our fast-paced culture, fast food is a daily reality for many young professionals. Eating around a table in a home with others is more likely a weekly, rather than a daily, practice. Today working parents, many single parent families, many young professionals and students eat on the go (often literally in the car). It is not unusual for modern families to possess no dining/ kitchen table in their home.

We prepared six young couples for marriage one summer and it was interesting to see the number of young university graduates who had never eaten together as a family while growing up. One young man commented on the fact that until being introduced to faith and church life, he had not known what it was like to share food with others. Eating had always been a purely functional and individual affair. It was very foreign to begin dating his girlfriend who came from a Christian home and who possessed two 'eating tables' – one in the dining room and another in the kitchen – where conversation and communication were paramount. He loved experiencing this new way of life. In beginning a new family, he was planning to be intentional about reviving this age-old practice in his own home. Studies regularly show how many times a family eats around a table will determine success at school, avoidance of anxiety, addictions and other identity-related disorders.

Invitations to Tuesday tea

This is where the Church can be a solution and play a fundamental role. Eating together is central to our faith and heritage, however foreign it is to culture today. In our own home we have found that an open-table culture where we regularly include young people is hugely attractive to young adults. Modern family life is so busy and, if we are honest, this family value is regularly threatened. Each evening we might be juggling working late and the taxi service of getting children to their various clubs/activities. It is a huge effort to get the immediate family in the same place at the same time, let alone extend the invitation to others.

In our own house, it helped us to make a practical decision to have at least one evening of the week where we commit to opening up our table to others. For several years, the Allan family has had a regular rhythm of 'Tuesday tea' where others will eat with us. We invite single people who might otherwise eat alone on other occasions to enjoy the blessing of banter and a loud table of teenagers! We invite teenage friends of our children with working parents, many of whom will rock up several times a week. We invite people who have appeared at our church and are new to the city, and therefore know no one. Urban life can be so lonely.

We also deliberately invite young adults and students that we are keen to have in our orbit. Those who might benefit from being introduced to 'family'. Those who God is asking us to deliberately spend time with. Leaders of the future and/or ones who might benefit from homely love and our occasional wisdom. Some of our very best discipleship happens around our range cooker and our kitchen sink.

You get to raid the fridge, but you do the washing-up

This way of life is only possible by straight talking and clear boundaries. We are so grateful to the families who opened up their homes to us when we were in our twenties. Around those kitchen tables we processed our theology, our callings, who we would marry, who we would vote for, how to avoid having an affair and those grown-up things of life that we otherwise did not have a natural context to speak about.

These families also modelled to us the practice of this way of life. We were generously invited to help ourselves to their food, but we knew that in exchange we needed to be willing to help these very busy families to function smoothly. We could offer to babysit, help with the DIY and so on. Our family now operates along similar lines; the same people who raid the fridge or enjoy a meal also get asked to do the washing-up. That's family!

I long to be part of family

The majority of research about Generations Y and Z has concluded that although they have witnessed the greatest breakdown in family structures they are now, paradoxically, the most family centric of all four previous generations. Granny's birthday must not be missed!

The emerging adults in our church really enjoy the company of older people; this is in stark contrast to our Generation X who saw themselves as 'different' and sought to distance themselves from the mainstream and the old. Generations Y and Z notably enjoy spending time with their parents, doing things like going on holidays together as teenagers or twenty-somethings. In our day, you turned eighteen and you planned your own summer – anything else would not have been cool.

Because this generation longs for a sense of family, whether they are Christians or not, they will often create support networks of pseudo families that offer the sort of social and emotional support they desire. How wonderful that at the heart of the Christian faith is 'a Father to the fatherless' (Ps. 68:5) and an invitation to 'come home'.

No complete families here!

Sometimes we use the metaphor of family for the local church, but we are aware that some of the single people in our congregation struggle with this. Perhaps it is because it doesn't feel like enough of a family to them, or perhaps because it makes them feel incomplete or inadequate not to be married with children. As an only child growing up in an Irish culture surrounded by huge extended families all appearing to have fun together, Marjorie knows how painful it can feel to long to be part of family. Interestingly, we have found that opening up our home to others has enriched our family. We are never self-sufficient!

In our early years of parenting, we soon realised that we were at a disadvantage not to have any grandparents living in our city. So we actively recruited some! We discovered that a lovely middle-aged couple in our church were grieving the loss of their family who had moved abroad, so we asked them to be surrogate grandparents for us. Our children today are all the richer from the young and the old who have helped shaped their lives and values; from our adopted-grannies who kindly babysat and even came on holiday with us, to the young people who lived in our home for a season. It is a beautiful picture of heaven's version of the home.

Case Study:

Charlotte (age twenty-seven) – family around the table

'What did you do at school today?' my mum says. It's a familiar question that I'm asked almost daily as I sit around the dining table with my family. As an excitable child, my words would fall over themselves as I shared everything I'd learned at school that day and all of the new people I had played with. As a teenager, I'd mutter something ambiguous, not wanting to be reminded of the friend I'd fallen out with during lunch hour.

These mealtimes were a consistent feature in my childhood. A regular rhythm of connection throughout my growing-up years. A picture of what it was to be a family. Because whether I felt like sharing that day or not, the simple act of sitting together, eating together and showing an interest in one another was enough to remind me that this unit was a place where I belonged, a place where people wanted to know *me*.

It was against this backdrop that I moved 200 miles away to university. Desperate to find a new place of belonging, I struggled with profound homesickness and loneliness. Although it often felt like it, I wasn't alone in feeling alone. The National Union of Students say that 50-70 per cent of students will feel homesick.[77] Following university, I found myself moving to Sheffield for work. It was clearly a call from God, so why did I still feel so lonely? As I tried to put down roots in this alien city, I couldn't help but notice that the loneliness was still there.

Millennials are a nomadic generation, moving from place to place for study, work, relationships, and as we do so we yearn for belonging. Sherry Turkle, in her 2012 TED Talk 'Connected, but Alone?'[78] argues that technology is exciting but it's changing us, making us so accustomed to being constantly connected that we crave this at all times. Perhaps that plays a part, but I think there's something more to it. We are built in the image of a triune God: Father, Son and Holy Spirit; three persons that are in relationship with each other. We are designed not to be alone but to belong. We are built for family.

Organisations have cottoned on to this — they describe their employees with familial language to create cultures of familial belonging. If you work at Google, you're a Googler; if you work at Pixar, you're a Pixarian. They've discovered the power behind belonging. But this isn't something new. The Bible paints a beautiful picture of lives shared, in all their messiness and in all their glory — that's what we see the first community of believers doing in Acts 2:42-47. And this community wasn't a group based merely on association, joined together because of a shared hobby or hometown. This was a group of people with a much deeper, common union.

In 2019, I felt a deep stirring from God to begin a community (house group) through our local church with the DNA of Romans 15:7 which is to 'welcome one another as Christ has welcomed you' (ESV). We've thought about what it means to be a family, to provide a place of belonging, warmth, inclusivity and hospitality. As we've done so, we've found God drawing people to us that are new to church or newly returning to church. We often don't know where they're at with God, or if they will ever set foot inside a church again. So we try to be as welcoming as we can in the moment, offering a place of family for those who want it.

On Sundays and in our everyday encounters this looks like being aware of people who are by themselves, and choosing to begin a conversation with them. It means inviting them with no pressure to join us one Wednesday evening. And on a Wednesday that looks like providing a safe space for people to be themselves. It means cooking a nice meal for people who often rely on their microwave because cooking for one is too much effort. It means exploring the Bible in an accessible way for anyone who may have joined us that week, giving space for questions, and opening ourselves up in the process. And if we see them again, we do exactly the same. If we don't, we pray for them anyway.

Each and every one of us longs for connection. We desire that safe place where we will be accepted. We want to be known. As Christians we have an amazing message of a God who loves us and values us and invites us into relationship with Him. We should never tire of sharing this. But sometimes, words aren't enough. Sometimes, actions speak louder. When I bought my first house last year as a single girl, I had a wishful dream-list of three bedrooms, sun-trap garden, walk-in wardrobe and much more. There was one thing, however, that was a non-negotiable: I wanted room for an extendable dining room table. I knew that my house was to be a place of family, of food eaten and of lives shared. And so, today, when I invite people into my home, I hope that it isn't just my words that speak of family. I hope that my home is a place that speaks for itself. A place that says: 'There is always room for you around my table.'

Today, Millennials are moving further from home, getting married later (if at all), and choosing when, how and if they have children. There has not been a better time for the Church to provide a place of belonging for all those that yearn for it, a place that mirrors that first community of believers in Acts 2.

As society redefines family, I think it's time for the Church to rediscover it.

74. Matthew 26:17-30.

75. *Leonard Sweet*, From Tablet to Table: Where Community is Formed and Identity Is Found (Colorado Springs, CO: NavPress, 2014), p. 9.

76. Survey conducted by Organix in conjunction with *The Telegraph*. Sally Peck, 'British Familes Don't Eat Together.' *The Telegraph*, Telegraph Media Group, 20 February 2013, www.telegraph.co.uk/women/mother-tongue/9882717/British-familes-dont-eat-together-and-if-they-do-its-often-in-front-of-the-TV.html (accessed 5.12.19).

77. National Union of Students, 'Homesickness can affect anyone', *nus.org.uk*, 20 September 2012, https://www.nus.org.uk/en/lifestyle/homesickness-can-affect-anyone/ (accessed 11.03.2020)

78. Sherry Turkle, TED Talk '*Connected, but Alone?*' TED, February 2012, retrieved from www.ted.com/talks/sherry_turkle_connected_but_alone (accessed 5.12.19)

CHAPTER TWELVE

We Want the Kingdom Without the King

There are only two kinds of people in the end: those who say to God, 'Thy will be done,' and those to whom God says, in the end, 'Thy will be done.' All that are in Hell, choose it. Without that self-choice there could be no Hell. No soul that seriously and constantly desires joy will ever miss it. Those who seek find. Those who knock it is opened.

(C.S. Lewis)[79]

A call to make Jesus Lord as well as friend

Everyone wants the eternal life which Jesus offers, even His enemies. 'But the gateway to life is very narrow and the road is difficult' says Jesus (Matt. 7:14). Far fewer people welcome the devotion and disciplines that keep our feet firmly on that road. Receiving unconditional love is a hugely popular concept in today's culture. Selfless submission in relationships and preferring others, the picture which the apostle Paul paints of Christian living in Ephesians chapters 5 and 6, well, that tends to be less popular in our post-Christian individualistic culture.

What do we mean in our description of a post-Christian culture? Much of our Western world continues to be influenced by Judeo-

Christian principles, whether it is aware of it or not.[80] While post-Christian culture is a reaction against and a deconstructing of what has been, it is not a return to ground zero. Post-Christian culture is often deeply spiritual, it yearns for justice and peace and often retains aspects of faith. In other words, much of the values and principles of Christianity remain at the centre of our culture's aspirations and the values by which most people practically live their lives. It is just that Christ Himself seems to have been airbrushed out. As author Mark Sayers observes: 'Post-Christian culture attempts to retain the solace of faith, whilst gutting it of the costs, commitments and restraints that the gospel places upon the individual will.'[81]

While Generations Y and Z may be increasingly nervous of the concept of absolute truth, they are very interested in doing good. So, what do they consider is good? Feeding the homeless – that's good. Caring for the environment – that's good. Racial inclusion – that's good.

Therefore, the socio-political vision of Jesus is good. What did Jesus do? He loved the poor, the widows and the orphans, He spoke out against injustice and spoke truth to political powers. He embodied justice, peace and equality. Very few people today would denounce these qualities of Jesus.

The rejection, therefore, is not of the entire gospel message. Often it is not even a rejection of Christ but of the messenger herself: the Church. We have under-represented the radical gospel of the kingdom to our neighbours for decades.

But Jesus' vision and invitation to the new world that He spoke of more than anything else was an invitation to the Kingdom of God (Mark 1:15). Few people would reject wanting the things of the kingdom – healing, wholeness or compassion – but many people, including some of those inside the Church as well as outside of it, reject surrendering their lives to the King of the kingdom. This is not even a simple paradox, this is a plain deception. 'Kingdom' means the King's rule or domain – the place where the King is in full authority.

It is actually impossible to have the fullness of kingdom and not surrender to the King.

Contemporary culture always longs for societal change, improvement and transformation. So far, so good. It is culture's misguided, or at best incomplete, prescription as to how that might happen which needs to be understood and clearly explained to young adults. The church we lead at present has a vision to serve our city of Sheffield, to work for good, to bring life to our city and ultimately to see the transformation of our city. The Buddhist commune down the road might have a similar vision to work for good. Rather than seeking personal transformation in Jesus Christ, our culture seeks societal transformation as a means to the end.

In a kingdom there is a king. When we are in the kingdom of God, we are in the King's domain. It is His property and things happen on His terms. Throughout the Scriptures God is described as Lord, which means Master and Sovereign Ruler.

The kingdom without the king is a falsity and a façade both at a personal and societal level. As much as we may individually be drawn to the blessings of heaven, we cannot get away from the simple fact that the entry point to receive His life is to be willing to lose our own.

Many people may work for good in society, but only Jesus can fix the human heart by enveloping us into His. We may tinker at the edges, but women and children continue to be abused, human and drug trafficking continues – evil is rife; only a submission to the King of the kingdom can transform a person from the inside out.

God as my buddy

We have spent the last twenty-five years in the charismatic Western Church. Worship music has evolved over that time. The songs we sing reflect the God we know and believe in. When we first entered the born-again[82] world, we were so struck that people were singing songs to Jesus like He was their close friend – how audacious, yet how wonderful and absolutely captivating! Today we sing songs on a whole different level. We sing to God intimately as a lover. It is shocking and powerful. The lyrics and theology of today's teaching on sonship and oneness as our identity have greatly deepened our own theology, relationships with God, and our faith. *But* God is not a teddy bear or my pet dog. He is not there to do what I desire and demand.

People, even unbelievers, often find that we want God's intervention. We want God to swoop down from heaven and fix things. What we have discovered increasingly over the years is that it is far more common for God to operate by incarnation, not intervention. He looks to move into my life, to take over, to take up residence, and from that place of lordship and intimacy to bring about inner transformation. Psalm 24:1 says: 'The earth is the LORD's, and everything in it.' He is always our Master: we have to learn how to make it so. The narrow road gives us access to life as it is meant to be – the vitality of physical and spiritual life which Jesus calls 'life to the full' in John 10:10.[83] This access to the kingdom, *His* kingdom, will squeeze my own kingdoms out of me. The broad road is full of deception, blind spots, excuses and false thinking.

Don't separate 'good' from 'God'

Jesus was a man of deep compassion and fervent passion. His life was constantly poured out for others, and following in the footsteps of Jesus will lead us down the same paths.

Conversely, we are surrounded today by a hugely individualistic society, and the highest good has now been redefined as individual freedom, happiness, self-expression. Anything or anyone that is seen to restrain or restrict any of the above becomes framed as an enemy of freedom.

Be aware – this kind of attitude wages war against discipleship.

In such a culture, social justice is increasingly seen to be rather less about economic or social equality and more about issues of equality relating to personal identity. Today as much as ever it is important for us to be very clear in this haze of ideas: we are sinners in need of a Saviour. The cross holds both love and justice together. At the cross those who recognise their sin collide with a Saviour. The exclusivity of the cross is the narrow gateway to the inclusivity of the Kingdom. There is no different path and the kindest thing is actually to make that really clear: both to new and existing Christians who seek to become genuine disciples.

I'd like to choose what's right and wrong for myself

Deep within every person is a longing for righteousness and justice. While these desires well up from within, we also want the right to choose what is right and wrong for ourselves.[84]

More than ever before, today's generations struggle with being told what to do and indeed with what to think. They have been commissioned to be in command of their world. Today we are surrounded by many young Christians who want the authority to rule their own kingdom and to judge for themselves. It would probably be fair to say that in many ways this has been the state of affairs since the Garden of Eden and there is nothing new here. What has shifted/gone is the foundation of a biblical world view, and biblical morality. Western society has historically been deeply shaped by a biblical world view; Barna's recent USA research on Generation Z highlights the fact that only 4 per cent of this generation have a biblical world view.[85]

Show me who the King really is and what it means to trust Him

In this post-Christian culture, it is therefore vital that we preach a compelling vision of our King. The King from whom beautiful justice and mercy flows. The King of right relationships. The forgiving Father. The Spirit who convicts us of sin, but never condemns us in heart. It is futile to try to persuade or train people in the value of a kingdom lifestyle who have not had a personal encounter with the King. It will only lead to frustration for them and judgement on our part when their behaviour fails to match our expectations.

Part of the tension of wanting to be in control lies in this generation's brokenness when it comes to trust. Who can blame them? Many have grown up without a father, or at least, not a residential one. Increasingly the parents of young adults and students are divorcing as they leave home, massively eroding their sense of trust and family. In Sheffield we frequently minister to young individuals who have fallen in love and who are naturally moving towards marriage, but for whom the commitment of marriage is really challenging on account of the breakdown in relationships, affairs and deceit that they have personally witnessed close at hand.

Many of today's current worship songs are a heart's cry response to this situation. Phrases enforcing the idea that God is not going to let us down, and titles like 'Who You Say I Am'[86] are a reflection of the anxious thoughts and experience of a generation, but are also a reflection of a King who is the very answer to this troubled world.

Once again, this is an opportunity for the Church to step forward and model a stronger image of family and healthy marriages and relationships, and to support those who set out to redeem their experience of family and marriage. Similarly, in our response to those in authority, the Church has an opportunity to counteract the emerging generation's general distrust towards institutional leadership, which only serves to fuel their individuality.

Don't mention death . . .

So why do you keep calling me 'Lord, Lord!' when you don't do what I say?'

(Luke 6:46)

Recently a young adult we are friends with wrote a social media post questioning the use of the word 'Lord' in reference to Jesus, because they found it 'old-fashioned' as an expression, with connotations of empire and paternalism. Yet, Jesus was unwavering in His presentation of the gospel: that it would cost us and that it involved taking up our cross to follow Him. Repeatedly, He outlines the fact we cannot have two masters (see Matt. 6:24).

Submission and the lordship of Christ are not necessarily attractive to anyone. Let's face it, death is never attractive. No one ever voluntarily chooses death unless they have the same vision before them as took Jesus to the cross: 'For the joy that was set before him' (Heb. 12:2). The question a church leader or mentor must ask is this: 'Am I living this way?' A white-hot vision of Jesus in our preaching, in our personal lives, is therefore vital if we are to be used by God in shaping culture and transforming others. This can often be a huge personal challenge to us. If we are on fire, others will find it much easier to find themselves caught up in the blaze. If apathy surrounds us then we may potentially be part of the problem. After all, we are asking them to 'imitate me, just as I [rather poorly] imitate Christ'.[87]

Such a mindset has helped Marjorie to keep her heart soft as a leader of young people. She remembers a few years ago she was struggling internally with the fact that she could see that very few of our young adult congregation had learned to tithe their money to the local church and to welcome Jesus' ownership of 100 per cent of their finances. Then the Holy Spirit showed her that perhaps she might actually be the one to blame for failing to train them well. Specifically, we were teaching and training in generosity but not speaking clearly about the tithe. She repented personally and publicly, searched the Scriptures for clarity and truth and began passionately teaching on tithing. There was a significant response among the young people in terms of their financial giving, and God had dealt with her judgement.

Let us not forget – discipleship usually begins with me! Obedience is at the very heart of our friendship with God.

I'm not wise enough! If He's the landlord, He covers the bills

As the battle in our individualistic society rages and we live in the centre of it, it can feel really overwhelming to be in charge of your own life. Yet, that is what our world tells us to do. I must follow my dreams, find my form of self-expression at all costs, fight for my life and my rights, not give over control to anyone at any cost. 'This is Me' is the title of the hugely popular song from *The Greatest Showman,* but its sentiments are blatantly anti-gospel.[88]

School leavers are told to follow their own desires, chart their own course, follow their dreams and 'find yourself'. Sadly, the same advice can be echoed from the popular pulpits of our nations. Jesus actually said the opposite – you want to find your life, you have to lose it (see Matt. 10:39). This is ultimate freedom – it is such good news! Why? Because I am not wise enough to be in control. If I am the owner of the house, I'm responsible when it all goes wrong – but if He is the landlord, He's responsible for the plan of rescue and redemption.

As we learn how to put this into practice in our everyday lives the concept of 'freedom' takes on a whole new meaning. It is no longer defined by Church traditions in reference to the style of worship or the gender of leadership. It is no longer defined by me. Real freedom grows as I learn to follow Him by asking, 'What is God saying and what will I do about it?' In other words, how am I obeying and changing? As the psalmist says, 'Take delight in the LORD, and he will give you your heart's desires' (Ps. 37:4).

Real transformation – is it actually possible?

Anyone who has any experience of pastoring people will have encountered the frustrating tendency of humans to make decisions to change and then to make foolish ones to return to their old ways. Perhaps this is less toxic than those in today's culture that have not even noticed that any change is required at all. Often their self-centred viewpoint is supported by their personal echo chamber of loud voices affirming their behaviour or feelings.

Perhaps it is more honest to say that many people are internally self-loathing, or so frustrated with themselves that they find it convenient and easier to avoid the facts by talking about the faults, failures and stereotypes of others.

All this begs the question: can we actually change?

The answer is yes! But probably in not the way we first imagine.

We change as we follow *in the footsteps of Jesus.*

It takes a lifetime, it lasts beyond. It is not simply adhering to a set of ideas, doctrines or ethics. It is a practice. Although today we live in an instant culture, there are no short cuts with Jesus. If we truly wish to partake of the life Jesus offers, we must also partake of the lifestyle. The lifestyle of Jesus, learning radically to follow Him in His words, ways and wonders is where true life and freedom may be found.

> Can one blind person lead another? Won't they both fall into a ditch? Students are not greater than their teacher. But the student who is fully trained will become like the teacher.
>
> *(Luke 6:39-40)*

We are all disciples of something

We are all shaped by culture and other people. My teenagers are shaped, for example, by today's vloggers. They watch, they are enticed, fascinated, they imitate. This should be a wake-up call that discipleship is not a church thing or just a religious thing. It is part of what it means to be human. It is a human thing to follow someone, or something else – that is how we are hardwired. Much as we might believe we are individuals, we are made and shaped to follow. Perhaps more than ever before in history, culture today is full of followers, principally generated by the power and reach of social and news media. We follow people's lives, conversation threads, consumer choices, political discussions.

But we are created primarily to follow our Maker in deep friendship and to be shaped by the Potter, our heavenly Dad (Isa. 64:8). He does it so well. We are invited to follow a speaking, acting, moving, creative, inventive God.

He initiates and we respond.

He is the King and I am not.

It has been like that since Eden and there has been no change of plan, and no alternative options have been offered by God. We are simply called to learn how to be with Jesus in devotion; to become like Him in response to His grace and challenge to our characters, and from that place of secure devotion, to do the things that Jesus did.

---

79. THE GREAT DIVORCE by CS Lewis © copyright CS Lewis Pte Ltd 1946.
80. We have found reading or listening to material by Jordan Petersen very helpful for analysis.
81. Mark Sayers, *Disappearing Church* (Chicago, IL: Moody Publishers, 2016), p. 16.
82. See John 3:1-21.
83. NIV.
84. Genesis 3:1-7.
85. Barna Group and Impact 360 Institute, Gen Z: *The Culture, Beliefs and Motivations Shaping the Next Generation* (Ventura, California: Barna Group, 2018).
86. Ben Fielding and Reuben Morgan, 'Who You Say I Am'. Lyrics © Capitol Christian Music Group, Hillsong Worship 2018.
87. 1 Corinthians 11:1.
88. Benj Pasek and Justin Paul, *This is Me*, Los Angeles, Atlantic Records, 2017.

SECTION THREE

The Ways of this World

I have given them your word. And the world hates them because they do not belong to the world, just as I do not belong to the world. I'm not asking you to take them out of the world, but to keep them safe from the evil one. They do not belong to this world any more than I do. Make them holy by your truth; teach them your word, which is truth. Just as you sent me into the world, I am sending them into the world.

Jesus prays for His disciples, John 17:14-18

CHAPTER THIRTEEN

Truth in a Post-truth World

Being in a minority, even in a minority of one, did not make you mad. There was truth and there was untruth, and if you clung to the truth even against the whole world, you were not mad.

(George Orwell, Nineteen Eighty-Four)[89]

A gathering storm

A lie always harms another; if not some other particular man, it still harms mankind generally

(Immanuel Kant)[90]

The global financial crash of 2008 blighted the following generation to austerity. Perhaps worse still, as its underlying causes were exposed, what came to light was a shocking disregard for truth and a cover-up for the sake of self-interest that was symptomatic of a gathering storm, a growing trend within Western mindsets – a slide towards a post-truth world.[91] Today's emerging generations grew up in this atmosphere, whether they understood it or not. Sadly, this is only one example among many of lies and fraud emanating from those entrusted to uphold truth and probity.

Shifting ground

When we were children, the *Encyclopaedia Britannica* in multiple volumes was *the* ultimate source of truth, a repository of scholarship and the final word on knowledge. Begun in 1768 but last printed in 2010, it is virtually worthless now other than as an eBay curiosity. It was superseded by Wikipedia, written collaboratively by largely anonymous volunteers on the model of openly editable content.[92] Welcome to the postmodern world of academia and popular culture where there is no longer one fixed source or interpretation of truth, and every opinion is relative and open to 'editing' or reinterpretation. Is it an improvement? Arguably not. Teachers and universities prohibit Wikipedia's citation, and its founder Jimmy Wales admitted its content was seriously flawed as early as 2005.[93]

There are strong forces within culture which now propose that truth should be seen as relative, and traditional sources of orthodoxy or authority in truth and life are now often viewed with suspicion and resisted. More sinister still is the rise of 'alternative facts' and post-truth as a valid way of thinking, speaking, leading others and justifying actions. Add to this the rise of deliberate malicious lie-telling, misinformation and 'fake news' which is difficult to discern, and its pernicious impact impossible to measure.

That is not to say that truth is dead. Far from it. It remains that most people in Western society hold that some things are 'true' and truth does still prevail as a concept. It is fiercely defended by many including the influential news media whose function has traditionally been to expose and report truth and facts.

It is not that honesty is dead: what psychologists call 'truth bias' remains a fundamental component of human character. But it is now perceived as one priority among many, and not necessarily the highest. Sharing your innermost feelings, shaping your life drama, speaking from the heart: these pursuits are increasingly in open competition with traditional forensic values.[94]

Together we face a philosophical and cultural atmosphere that is increasingly incoherent and breeds mistrust and confusion among those authentically seeking the truth. 'What is truth?' asks Pontius Pilate (John 18:38) on behalf of a whole generation.

Leaders dethroned

Perhaps it is no wonder that Generations Y and Z have grown up to become broadly anaemic or resistant to 'experts'. They have been more exposed to news in this digital era than ever before. They are painfully aware of the brokenness and 'spin' of the world around them. It has bred a distrust of institutions and even the claim to authority and truth itself. They have witnessed the erosion of public trust in establishment figures as a series of scandals and exposes have revealed deeply cynical cover-ups, particularly in past ten years, with high-profile instances such as the Jimmy Savile scandal and BBC cover-up, the Cambridge Analytica and Facebook information scandal, or admissions of paedophilia within the established Church. As we seek to disciple people, we must be sensitive to this breakdown in trust for leadership, coupled with a dismantling of hierarchy across contemporary culture.

Alternative facts and post-truth

Into this mixed-up way of interpreting reality is growing a new trend which is extremely dangerous for society and Christian discipleship. In 2017 a White House spokesperson, Kellyanne Conway, rebuffed an NBC journalist's suggestion that her boss, the Press Secretary Sean Spicer, had lied about the numbers of people who attended President Trump's inauguration when calling it 'the largest audience ever to witness an inauguration, period, both in person and around the globe'.[95]

Conway's rebuff has gone down in history. She didn't view Spicer's comment as a lie. She wouldn't admit his numbers were false but simply 'alternative facts'. If everything is relative including the source of truth, then Sean Spicer's interpretation of reality suddenly and shockingly earned itself legitimacy. It was not deemed as wrong, but simply as alternative. This is a frightening extrapolation of our prevalent relativist philosophy.

Successful communication is now coming to rely less on the currency of facts or verifiable truth than on its ability to persuade and to win an emotional battle, to win people over. Another word for this is propaganda. The media, or any person, may now redefine reality by your 'facts' against my 'alternative facts'.

Most people still want truth and believe in facts. Today's danger is that we may be approaching what Orwell highlighted satirically as one of the worst crimes of totalitarian regimes: 'Doublethink'. 'Doublethink means the power of holding two contradictory beliefs in one's mind simultaneously, and accepting both of them.'[96] The problem is that when you choose your own reality without reference or convention, you also select your own falsehood.

Fake news

Another trend is further destabilising people's trust in truth. 'Fake news' is not a new phenomenon, but today the deliberate spreading of falsehood and disinformation seems to be seeping into our mainstream social media. The devil is the father of fake news. Jesus said the devil 'is a liar and the father of lies' (John 8:44), whose tactic is not so much to spread outright falsehood but rather to sow doubt.[97]

Regarding the fake news phenomenon, journalist Matthew d'Ancona says 'the trick is to provide disruptive entertainment as a distraction',[98] so that the conversation and disagreements simply roll on, rather than finding a conclusion in truth or fact.

Let me entertain you

What has risen in the place of an insistence on evidence-based approaches to determining the truth? What now seeks to fill the gap where rationality has retreated? Story. More than ever in perhaps the past 1,000 years, the power of story prevails. The place of 'meta-narratives' has gone – any single grand explanation for all of life's meaning is rejected, so that 'religion' is now treated much like the epic stories of Greek and Roman epic myths: deep and meaningful but not actually true.[99] But the power of simple, engaging stories is on the rise.

Two recent USA presidential campaigns have been won on the power of a story. It was Obama's audacity of hope which harnessed the grass-roots votes of the women, minorities and the young by his 'Yes We Can' slogan. In Trump's 2016 victory, the story of his campaign mattered arguably more than the facts. What captured the popular attention was a fanciful promise to 'Make America Great Again!' against the danger of 'crooked Hilary' and her Washington cronies. 'The effect was narcotic rather than rational', says one commentator.[100]

The key to influencing public opinion today lies in harnessing an emotional connection. It has always been part of decision-making, but today it has become so elevated that if 'it feels right' then it basically is counted as right. This is emotional evaluation. We are in danger of making decisions based upon popularity not substance, traction before truth. Not exclusively, of course, but the fact of the matter is seriously in danger of being overtaken by the feeling of the matter. 'Post-Trust is, first and foremost, an emotional phenomenon. It concerns our attitude to truth, rather than truth itself.'[101]

Platform power

What makes this possible is the rise of platform power. In a world of relativity, anybody with an opinion and a platform to share it instantly becomes elevated to the status of an expert. The dangers are clear: we now decide by picking sides rather than evaluating evidence. Whoever tells the best story, whoever shouts the loudest, or sings the sweetest now earns my vote, or attention, or even my devotion and destiny. The internet does not help; it allows equal access to the full range of opinions and is indifferent to truth and lies. Its algorisms tend to ignore complexity and subtlety. They encourage the confirmation bias of our personal echo chambers instead.

What is our response?

In today's prevailing culture we are heading towards a situation where as long as the stories *feel* true, then they resonate, and you may consider them to *be* true. If you hear the same thing repeated enough it becomes like 'truth' to you. Jesus spoke powerfully against this kind of deception:

> Your eye is like a lamp that provides light for your body. When your eye is healthy, your whole body is filled with light. But when your eye is unhealthy, your whole body is filled with darkness. And if the light you think you have is actually darkness, how deep that darkness is! No one can serve two masters. For you will hate one and love the other; you will be devoted to one and despise the other.
>
> *(Matt. 6:22-24)*

Confidence in the power of our story

How can Christians of every age group help our society at large to combat the worst dangers of this growing post-truth era?

Christians have an amazing story to tell! It is the antidote to today's hopeless narratives built upon disillusionment or confusion. We can be confident. We live a gospel that is incredibly powerful and empowering. With equal measures of humility and confidence, we have the opportunity to be culturally proactive, not always just culturally reactive – to disciple our prevailing culture with compassion and empathy. Where we have public platforms, we may set the tone and expectation, help people to interpret the times and evaluate reality.

We can speak out against false news and post-truth, but in a way that can be heard and received. Not just the dry facts – we must play the same communication game. Truth needs to be stated and repeated, but with an emotional delivery. Let us tell our story! It is powerful, emotive, but rooted in historical and eternal truth. We have to speak to head and heart at the same time. Jesus knew this when He said, 'Look, I am sending you out as sheep among wolves. So be as shrewd *as snakes* and harmless as doves' (Matt. 10:16).

The Church is commissioned to be a redemptive community. We believe that the Church can have a perfectly robust response to tensions within culture, for example by maintaining its integrity and orthodoxy in issues, but without holding a judgemental response, or an apparently uncomprehending or unsympathetic response. Nobody, especially the followers of our vastly creative, inventive, multifaceted God, needs to enforce absolute uniformity of views or faith. Nobody should claim to have the monopoly on the experience or interpretation of God. Sometimes the Church gets uppity and stuck on secondary rather than primary issues.

We are a missionary people, embodying Jesus' passion 'to seek and save those who are lost' (Luke 19:10). Many young adults just want to be listened to and heard properly a long time before we dare to point them towards an alternative lifestyle or world view such as Christianity represents. We ought to respond to society's confusions not with condemnation but with compassion. Compassion is better than sympathy or even empathy, because compassion seeks to intervene to bring about redemption. That will entail demonstrating great pastoral sensitivity and patience as we point people towards the love and truth of Jesus.

> ## Case Study:
>
> ### Wise Lives podcast (www.wiselives.co.uk)
>
> At The Well Sheffield we are embracing the podcast and video revolution which is now extremely popular with young adults. In 2019 we launched the Wise Lives podcast and video show:
>
> > Honest Conversations in under 30 minutes about the authentic Christian life in contemporary culture. The grit and the glory of how we seek first the kingdom of God in everyday life.[102]
>
> We talk openly about the challenges as well as the joys of following Jesus wholeheartedly. People appreciate when we are honest and authentic. Wise Lives is intended firstly to help to disciple our own church people, but also to speak to a generation. Like many Christians, we figured that since YouTube and podcasts are such a key way for young adults to receive information and entertainment, then the Church ought also to be vocal and attractive in this arena. After all, if we are not guiding the conversations in this space, then contemporary culture will be discipling people instead.
>
> Hosting content on the web or channels such as YouTube or Facebook is simple and often free. For the investment in some equipment, time and skills comes a potentially wide audience.

How do we disciple emerging adults in this context?

How do we disciple emerging adults in today's emerging post-truth context? Here are six ways to help people to navigate through the growing storm:

1. Tell a better story

2. Jesus is the only way – keep the Bible as the true foundation

3. Personal experience translated within community

4. Ask the deep questions

5. Learn to discern

6. The power of waiting and limitations

1. Tell a better story

Christians are ideally placed to tell a better, more compelling story than that of prevailing culture. Do not underestimate the power of the story you carry within your heart and life, the gospel that drips with goodness. It is the greatest story ever told and we know it ends well. Our young people experience such anxiety and disquiet, but the gospel speaks of hope and purpose. Let us call them towards a life of greatness, of empowered humility.

We have to operate within the current parameters of society. Facts are no longer enough. The ground has shifted, so our message and methods must adapt too. Emotional evaluation has risen to the top of the pile. Our approach must be emotionally intelligent, weaving facts alongside a compelling storyline. Isn't that what preachers have always done? Let us appeal to head and heart alike. Let us speak to the roots and the heart of the issue as we address real-life concerns. Emerging adults applaud and give platform to those they grow to trust and those who are true to themselves in integrity and authenticity. It is all about relationship-building, just as discipleship has always been.

The conversion growth at The Well Sheffield is partly attributed to the power of story. We train people to be able to explain who Jesus is and the work of the cross and we encourage them to share with people they know the everyday stories of God at work in their lives. We have testimonies and stories at almost every Sunday service as we hear how God is touching and changing lives within our congregations. This is very attractive to people and is instrumental in creating a faith culture. As we learn to tell the story of what Jesus has done for us, we help others to locate their own way-markers in their journey towards Jesus. What God can do for one person He can do for another. We promote stories of changed lives in our city's media, we share video documentaries on our website, and at significant outreach times, like our Christmas carol services, we always have live testimonies of transformation. It is difficult to argue with a person's own story.

2. Jesus is the only way – the Bible is the true foundation

Times change, but Jesus remains 'the way, the truth, and the life'. In our discipleship, it is vital that we do not compromise on Jesus being truth, and the only way to the Father. Jesus is utterly unique. He says, 'I am the way' (John 14:6). This actually closes every other way to salvation. There is a tremendous invitation because Jesus *is* the answer to all of life's questions, and we can encourage and teach people in how to know and hear God for themselves by the Holy Spirit who will 'lead [them] into all . . . truth' (John 16:13 GNT). At the same time, we must resist the urge to control the outcomes!

Telling a better story does not mean we switch from a higher call for commitment and self-sacrifice to a pitch that promises immediate obvious benefits without mentioning perseverance and character change. Like Jesus, we are aiming to build resilient disciples. Discipleship is about going deep, not shallow. We may come with honesty and expectation of glorious transformation.

We must help young adults in learning to read the Bible and learning to trust in it as the greatest source of truth about God and humanity. Get it into their hands (not just their phones) and grapple together with how to best to interpret and apply it for today. Many emerging adults doubt the truth or reliability of the Bible, partly because they do not understand how it was compiled, or they get stuck on its apparent contradictions or 'old-fashioned' attitudes. Do not assume that even those who grew up within church/Sunday school actually feel confident in handling the texts. Instead, find engaging ways to inform and equip them to read and interpret it themselves, and alongside their peers.

At The Well Sheffield we run a short course regularly called 'Bible Basics' to equip Christians in how to understand, interpret and apply the Bible. We also expect all of our weekly community groups in people's houses to use the Discovery Bible Study[103] method to read and apply Bible passages. It is a flexible, group-based format designed to draw people into the interaction of Scripture with their lives. We find it to be very accessible to the unchurched, as well as encouraging obedience and discipleship in Christians.

Case Study:

Rachel's experience of Bible Basics (age thirty-seven)

I really valued doing the Bible Basics course because I want to further my relationship with Jesus. I know that the more I understand His Word then the closer that relationship will become, but I don't often know where to start with handling the Bible. The course helped me to appreciate the context when reading the Bible so that I could apply the ancient stories and teachings to my everyday life. And I really appreciated getting to talk through what we were learning about with the other people doing the course – it felt great to be able to talk about my questions too in a supportive environment.

3. Personal experience translated within community

Many emerging adults rank their personal experience as the highest indicator of truth, or what to trust as accurate, authentic, authoritative. This can work to our advantage in discipleship by encouraging people to find their own relationship with God, at a deep personal level. Encourage personal encounter through the power of the Spirit, who is the greatest discipler and can be trusted to '*guide you* into *all truth*' (John 16:13, italics ours).

But the best kind of theology develops in community.[104] When Jesus discipled His followers, He very rarely did it alone, He did it among a trusted, like-minded small community. We have found that being a committed member of a trusted small group-sized community provides emerging adults with the safest foundation to process life and questions of discipleship. A peer group of Christians will hopefully even out the effect of pick 'n' mix theology, by challenging and debating the more extreme ends of people's opinions. Those who seek to disciple emerging adults must walk alongside them, through their highs and lows, helping them to navigate by identifying the work of the Holy Spirit in their lives, and prompting them to come to conclusions fully informed by faith.

The danger is that we embrace isolation and we do our own personalised theology aside from community and accountability. We're heard it described this as 'Google theology' which provides easy access to those people who will confirm your prejudices or existing errors. But Christian theology is best established in accountable Christian community.

4. Ask the deep questions

Helping emerging adults to seek truth and be true to Jesus' ways is vital. It is not enough to know about the truth. People need to be helped to assess their own lives, mindsets, decisions, choices against the benchmark of Jesus as revealed principally through the Bible. How is biblical truth and God's character and expectations fitting into and moulding my everyday behaviour and character?

'Blessed are all who hear the word of God and put it into practice' (Luke 11:28). Jesus' model is mindset change. 'Repent ... and believe the Good News' (Mark 1:15) may be interpreted as 'change your mind' (*metanoia)* and 'step out in faith' (*pistis*) in your new revelation. Once a person has encountered God, we should help them to assess which of their prevailing mindsets or truths Jesus is challenging to change in the light of His new revelation to them. Then we accompany them in dismantling the old way of thinking, or the captivity to the old nature/self and aligning their thinking and action to the truth in Jesus.

> Thank God! Once you were slaves of sin, but now you wholeheartedly obey this teaching we have given you. Now you are free from your slavery to sin, and you have become slaves to righteous living.
>
> *(Rom. 6:17-18)*

Deep discipleship means encouraging reflective practice in people. Helping them to think carefully, from a godly perspective, on all issues of life and then to act in a way that is true to their convictions and the revelation God will give.

In a culture which prizes asking the big questions, many young people we know are hungry for deep answers. This should be encouraged and helped. We are often struck by the inquisitive minds in our midst who hunger for answers of substance to their perfectly normal questions about Church history, theology, the Scriptures and the nature of the Church herself. There has never been an easier era in which people may locate further resources to dig deeper.

5. Learn to discern

We are aiming to help emerging adults to be very discerning in where they find their source of authority, their models for life and thought. Today's trendy internet vloggers are better placed to disciple my children in everyday opinions than I may be. They have access direct to my own teenage children's devices, and a platform to influence the whole world. The problem is, they are often peddling a brand of pick 'n' mix pop-psychology and morality that is miles away from Jesus' way. It is absolutely vital that we equip emerging adults in discernment. What are the values or motivations that are bombarding them from the web, their peers, their education or entertainment? Where is the truth, where is the lie or the ungodly morality which presents itself so appealingly? What ideas are being shared and reposted without due diligence? Our family plays a game during long car journeys called Spot the Lie. We ask the children to dissect the subtle messages portrayed on advertising billboards. What lies or manipulations are masquerading in seductive images or words?

It is often not as simple as discerning between obvious right and wrong. The power of story or the shiny packaging of social media can sugar-wrap a detrimental untruth. And people tend to trust what they like, what makes them feel good. As George Orwell observed in his book *Nineteen Eighty-Four*: 'The choice for mankind lies between freedom and happiness and for the great bulk of mankind, happiness is better.'[105]

Discernment requires some hard thinking and slowing down. Discernment means looking beyond our personalised house of mirrors and echo chamber or our natural individualism. Training in discernment means we do not accept the premise of every proposition, however much we might be attracted to it.

6. The power of waiting and limitations

Life for a young adult can fly at 100 miles an hour. This is the instant generation, who demand an instant fix and immediate results, having little patience for 'process' or gradual development (except, we've noticed, for home brew). We see this in pastoral care, and lately a Christian GP told me she has experienced just the same attitude in her consulting rooms among these generations. Experiencing limits and limitations, having to wait for something, coming up against a boundary marker: none are popular with young adults – yet they may be just the medicine they require.

Help a person to avoid the crippling paralysis of multichoice by actively choosing to slow down and smell the coffee. To embrace the need to stop. Simply to breathe a little and take stock of events. To wait a while. As Jesus recommends, to 'deny' yourself for a while (Matt. 16:24, NIV).[106] Wisdom shows that it is through being denied or failing that a person can truly grow the most in their character and spirituality, if only they would embrace the process and not buck at it. Nobody can teach this; a person has to experience it for themselves – but a wise mentor can at least make people aware of these truths and prepare them through occasional practice.

There is a lot to be said for the ancient holy habits, or spiritual discipline practices.[107] Emerging adults may love the disciplines of engagement, such as worship, celebration and meeting together. In a fast-paced world which often lacks a depth of discernment, it is the disciplines of abstinence which may hold the key to finding truth.

'Jesus said to his disciples, "If any of you wants to be my follower, you must give up your own way, take up your cross, and follow me"' (Matt. 16:24).

Emerging adults are prone to significant digital distractions and experience almost continuous intrusions into their thought-space. They have learned multitasking as a result, but the flip side is a chronic lack of solitude and of genuine inner-work. Of course, this has been typical of young adults for centuries; it is not a specifically new issue, but it is a particularly pressing and pernicious one for the twenty-first century.

'Our much-discussed crisis of distraction today is, put differently, a crisis of solitude. We don't want to disconnect, even though indulging screen time instead of stillness is taking a toll on our mental health. We know that, in contrast, measured idleness is good for us and can actually catalyze creative breakthrough.'[108]

SEVEN DEADLY SINS OF 21ST CENTURY

(from *Player One* by Douglas Coupland)[109]

1. Willingness to accept information overload
2. Neglect of the maintenance of democracy
3. Deliberate ignorance of history
4. Equating of shopping with creativity
5. Rejection of reflective thinking
6. Belief that spectacle is reality
7. Vicarious living through celebrities

Case Study:

When the smartphone goes. Ronan (age thirty-seven), young offenders prison chaplain

On a weekly basis in my young offenders' prison we see many young men surrender their lives to Jesus, experiencing the power of God and going on to attend discipleship groups.

The two challenges I see for young adult discipleship today are the absolute importance of the Word of God being our total authority, and people's addiction to instant entertainment, in particular smartphones.

One of the things that prison does is to strip men of their comforts, community and all that seems familiar. This includes access to smartphones and modern technology. These devices can be wonderful and fun but they often fill and consume people's lives so that it takes over their desire to seek and follow Jesus. It is in the stripping away of all of these that men realise their desperate need for God and a desire for Him that they never knew was there.

We often want the life Jesus lived but don't always want to do what He did in order to do this. The need to declutter our lives and be disciplined in what we are doing with our time is so important to this generation. It is in this decluttering that getting the Word of God into us is so important.

As other distractions are removed, I see hungry young men choosing to take up the cause of Christ in prison – one of the world's toughest environments. When they realise how much they need God they then develop a love for Scripture and taking its direction on everyday decisions. This generation needs to rediscover a love for God's Word and to choose to make it their ultimate authority in their lives again and to seek His face with the same passion with which we seek entertainment and pleasure.

89. George Orwell, *Nineteen Eighty-Four* (London: Penguin Classics, New Ed., 2004).
90. Immanuel Kant, *Critique of Practical Reason and Other Writings in Moral Philosophy*, ed. and trans. Lewis White Beck (Chicago, IL: University of Chicago Press, 1949), pp. 346-350.
91. For some years, particular parts of the US money markets which drive the world's financial system had been internally fraudulent. Their regulators pretty much knew it and ignored it. They traded in certain products that contained 'sub-prime mortgages' which were essentially worthless liabilities. Regulators did nothing to restrict the products or their trade, while ratings agencies certified them 'AAA' for a long time after their true n ature had been exposed. It was a colossal untruth and the result was a near catastrophe on a global scale, which Britain and others has not recovered from over a decade later.
92. https://en.wikipedia.org/wiki/Wikipedia:About (accessed 6.12.19).
93. Andrew Orlowski, 'Wikipedia Founder Admits to Serious Quality Problems', *The Register*, 18 October 2005, www.theregister.co.uk/2005/10/18/wikipedia_quality_problem/ (accessed 6.12.19).
94. Matthew d'Ancona, *Post Truth: The New War on Truth and How to Fight Back* (London: Ebury Press, 2017), p. 34.
95. Elle Hunt, 'Trump's Inauguration Crowd: Sean Spicer's Claims versus the Evidence', *The Guardian*, Guardian News and Media, 22 January 2017, www.theguardian.com/us-news/2017/jan/22/trump-inauguration-crowd-sean-spicers-claims-versus-the-evidence (accessed 6.12.19).
96. Ibid. See endnote 90.
97. To Eve the serpent sows doubt, 'Did God really say ...?' (Gen. 3:1) To Jesus the devil questions what His Father had already spoken over Him, 'If you are the Son of God ...' (Matt. 4:3).
98. Ibid. See endnote 94.
99. The power of epics remains surprisingly palatable in the fantasy superhero realm of Marvel movies. The biggest grossing movie of its time, *Endgame* (2019) is a simple story of good vs evil, the weak vs the strong, a malevolent personality (Thanos) acting like Satan to collect all power to himself and destroy an ignorant civilisation, while the heroes strive against all odds to save the planet from destruction.
100. Matthew d'Ancona, *Post Truth: The New War on Truth and How to Fight Back* (London: Ebury Press, 2017), p. 15.
101. Ibid. See endnote 94, p. 126.
102. www.wiselives.co.uk (accessed 8.2.20).
103. See Appendix 2 for more information.
104. Mark 8:14-21, for example.
105. Ibid. See endnote 89.
106. Interestingly, one subculture within young adults is very good at appreciating the need to stop and recover periodically: the body builders. These strong men know that their muscles grow and strengthen only through rest, not through continual work. I often hear them in my gym when a friend asks, 'Are you in tomorrow?' saying, 'No, mate, it's a recovery day! I'll be back in a couple of days' time.' If they can appreciate the rewards of limits and waiting in the gym, why not in all aspects of life?
107. For two great resources, see Dallas Willard's classic book, *The Spirit of the Disciplines* (San Francisco, CA: HarperSanFrancisco, 1991) and Richard J. Foster, *Celebration of Discipline* (London: Hodder & Stoughton, 2008).
108. Andy Olsen, 'Fighting FOMO', ChristianityToday.com, *Christianity Today*, 17 December 2019, www.christianitytoday.com/ct/2018/january-february/our-jan-feb-issue-fighting-fomo.html (accessed 5.12.19).
109. Douglas Coupland, *Player One: What is to Become of Us* (London: William Heinemann, 2010). Adapted.

CHAPTER FOURTEEN

FOMO and YOLO:
Discernment in Decision-Making

We use the descriptor 'emerging adulthood' for good reason. It is a season of asking the big questions of life and of oneself, without necessarily coming to all the conclusions. As the scaffolding of adolescence falls away, people face an enormous variety of choices and potential. Today's generations seek whole-life balance because, after all, YOLO (You Only Live Once). But because of the complexity and transitory nature of contemporary life, and the competing values of contemporary culture, they will also often experience parallel periods of high anxiety on account of their very real FOMO (Fear Of Missing Out). They may struggle to take any decisions of lasting impact or investment.

Consider our changing times. In this accelerated world, it can be difficult to keep up with things. Take fashion, for example. International fashion used to run by seasons: winter and summer collections had a rhythm to their change. Today's digital world has led to fast-fashion where trends can rise and fall at any time. Keen followers of fashion today feel an unabating need to keep on top of trends, and then to manage their Snapchat streaks.

At times Generations Y and Z are caricatured as floaty, indecisive and lacking commitment. Sometimes that's unfair, instead they are simply exercising their freedoms and empowerment within a mobile culture, during a naturally transient season of emerging-adult life. Sometimes they really are floaty, paralysed by too much choice and too little time/money/purpose, and without the tools to discern a positive direction. Other times, there can be deep-seated mental health challenges which hinder this remarkably resilient generation from coping with the pace of this multiple-choice life.

Those seeking to disciple and mentor these generations can offer a very helpful toolset and mindset towards healthy, wise decision-making. Christian discipleship is about assisting people in their discernment and godly decision-making. Young adults in churches today carry a strong desire to connect with God and hear His voice, yet sometimes they lack a little wisdom and discernment. As the generations work together, we may empower young adults to navigate these unchartered waters wisely and safely, so as to 'seek the Kingdom of God above all else' (Matt. 6:33).

The meaning of life

Soul II Soul famously asked what the meaning of life was when I was graduating university in 1996.[110] The music scene has moved on since then, yet today Kelly Clarkson is still asking what the meaning of life is, in a song which has been played 10 million times on Spotify.[111] Why? Because the fundamental questions remain the same.

As a person develops during their twenties and thirties, these questions find greater depth and meaning. Most twenty-somethings may not yet have developed too many answers, but in establishing their independent lives they are always asking, 'Where do I fit in?' and will daily be asking questions like 'How do I live well?', 'How do I navigate this multichoice world?', 'What does it mean to be an adult, and when did I become one?' If you are a Christian, then alongside these questions of life you typically also begin to question your faith in more detail, testing some of the assumptions you inherited from parents or leaders to see if they stand up to your expanding views and experience of the world.

Young adulthood is a crucial life stage when aspects central to any person, such as world view and values, are established through testing, and foundations are laid upon which the rest of life is built. Sociologist Jeffrey Arnett[112] identifies three universal criteria markers of entering adulthood:

1. Accepting responsibility for yourself

2. Making independent decisions

3. Becoming financially independent

Emerging adulthood is a journey, a process of making various choices usually in these directions. It is a season of life characterised in part by instability and transitional or provisional connections. Most of the central aspects of life are in flux, or early stages of development: career, relationships, sexuality and for some, gender identity, even our body's physical capacity. Other big shifts include a person's perception of values and judgement amid a bewildering access to and speed of information, truth and fake news, cultural diversity, consumer choice and Christian choice (e.g. a variety of flavours of church to attend or draw from). In short, it is usually a time of mobility and transience. It is a world of choice, but making those choices can be very challenging.

> 'Studies agree that the transition to adulthood today is even more complex, disjointed, and confusing than it was in past decades. The steps through schooling, a first real job, marriage, and parenthood are simply less well organized and coherent today than they were in the past. At the same time, these years are marked by a historically unparalleled freedom to roam, experiment, learn, move on, and try again.'[113]

Occasionally people very deliberately make choices in an opposite direction, perhaps out of avoidance, fear or simply not feeling ready or equipped. Those seeking to help and disciple should be aware of the glorious positives and freedoms that young adults enjoy, like the untethered space to explore and invent, and also of how complex this season of life really is. Principally this is because life's sturdiest foundations have yet to be established.

> . . . infants, tossed back and forth by the waves, and blown here and there by every wind of teaching and by the cunning and craftiness of people . . .
>
> *(Eph. 4:14, NIV)*

Growing up slowly

Recently Nick asked a twenty-one-year-old girl what she planned do after graduating from university. Quite plainly, she said she was 'definitely not ready to get a job, and it's not the right time'. Instead, she was planning to move home to be able to be closer to her parents.

We also recently had dinner with a fifty-something couple from church whose early-twenties' children lived with them, holidayed together and still needed some financial support after university. Everybody was happy about it, even though it cramped their style somewhat and had meant the parents making unexpected choices to remain in work and in situ a bit longer than they had expected.

There is a common observation that today's young adults do not really grow up as rapidly as in generations past. At age eighteen we had both left home for university, and began to cut ourselves off from our parental nest and influence. Studies show that today nearly 1 million more young adults are living with their parents than was the case twenty years ago. Almost 26 per cent of twenty to thirty-four-year-olds did so in 2017.[114] Partly this is due to the brutal realities of the job market since 2008 and rocketing house prices. Partly, it is a reaction to the 'helicopter parenting' of their upbringing. Young adults don't want – or even see the need – to fend entirely for themselves or to take the kind of risks which previous generations did. Some think, 'Why would I leave home?' Others know that economically they have little other choice and yet aren't in a hurry to establish the kind of career which would lead to financial independence. Similarly, many parents welcome this extension of their time at home with their offspring.

This situation is not necessarily bad, but it is different. If you are a parent with young adults at home, try not to resent it but see the positive that you get to disciple your children for longer even though the boundary lines are much more blurred in terms of their self-reliance, growing up and taking responsibility.

Defeating the disease to please

Generations Y and Z are highly relational as people and are influenced and even defined by how others perceive or receive them. For a Christian seeking to make good, godly decisions, they find themselves trying to please God in this mix of pleasing yourself, while simultaneously trying to please others. This means that at times high stakes decisions can be reached quite spontaneously or chaotically, or even irresponsibly or selfishly. That is not unique to Generations Y and Z, it is simply a feature of twenty-something life as people mature to develop away from the natural self-centredness of youth.

'Who did you process that with?'

Once a man in his mid-twenties made the sudden decision to leave our church, cut ties with the city and move away. Over coffee, one of our young-adult leaders gently asked him who he had processed this decision with, and he enthusiastically replied, 'Nick and Marjorie!' The reality was that he had informed us of his already-taken decision, but he had not asked us our opinion, or indeed weighed any other options with us.

The opportunity for mentoring and discipleship is about assisting discernment and godly decision-making. Our experience is that emerging adults will frequently take decisions in isolation, without talking it over first in a way which invites genuine critique. They inform you *after* the decision or event has occurred, and miss the opportunity to discern their choices against kingdom of God values, with the help of wise counsel. We often find ourselves asking, 'And who did you process that with?' Increasingly, we find we need to clarify and qualify what we mean by this. Processing means taking time to reflect and discuss together; inviting others to speak into your life; enquiring 'What would they do if they were me?', praying together, seeking wise counsel. We seek to teach emerging adults to think in community before they act. This is different than simply chatting together!

'Help me to navigate my multi-choice world'

Choice is a big deal. Today's generations grow up with the greatest-ever menu set in front of them. Since childhood they have been invited into decision-making, from which after-school clubs they'd enjoy, to which TV show to select from multiple devices in our world of on-demand content. There are apps to help you choose a partner, there is the choice of 100 plus universities in the UK, there are choices to live and work abroad or at home.

There are many positives. These are generations known for their flexibility and ingenuity, refusing to be restricted by the norm. An expectation of change is part of their make-up. They develop an admirable resilience, having experienced rapid shifts in life since a young age, whether from neutral sources such as our technology revolution or negative ones like sudden parental break-ups. Sociologists identify this kind of common experience as VUCA – Volatility, Uncertainty, Complexity and Ambiguity[115] – and we ought to appreciate and support those who are developing within such a world.

Curiosity is king. Millennials in the workplace will want to know the value of any task they are asked to perform: 'Why should I invest my energy in it, and what's the big picture?' They are confident in asking questions and challenging assumptions.

Studies show that their average time in a job is now under two years (the total UK workplace average is five years[116]), and the gig economy of part-time or temporary jobs has become a lifestyle choice, not simply a 'McJob' means to get by. In fact, researchers suggest that the average Generation Z may occupy a total of seventeen jobs, and five different careers, across their lifetime.[117] They work flexibly and are blurring the traditional work/life boundaries. 'Job satisfaction' was something Gen X craved. Today it's 'life satisfaction' and 'whole-life balance'[118] as work, relationships, and quality of life vie for balance, and emerging adults crave the feeling that they are appreciated for their contributions. They hold a higher expectation of gaining satisfaction in life, in work, relationships, entertainment and so forth. A KPMG report observes: 'It's simple – if millennials don't see the opportunity to move up, they move out.'[119]

'Don't stand back and watch me implode'

This means that anyone who belongs to Christ has become a new person. The old life is gone; a new life has begun!

(2 Cor. 5:17)

Over the years we have seen Christians make some pretty odd, irrational or even dangerous decisions. We have counselled them to act in one direction, and seen people walk determinedly in the opposite direction. Why? Was our advice so bad?

A person's decision-making process is driven by deep-lying motivations and patterns of belief about the world, about God, about themselves. Sometimes they may be almost unaware of these and they will need some deliberate help to dig deeper. The process of discipleship is one of intentionally rerouting our souls (mind, body, emotions) to catch up with the reality of our spirits. In other words, Christians are *already* adopted children of God, beloved and forgiven in their heavenly Father's eyes, and commissioned to impact this world for the kingdom of God. When you become a Christian, you are 'new creation' – that means 'the old is gone' (2 Cor. 5:17, GNT). It is just that we forget that sometimes. We cannot keep it front-of-mind in our everyday lives; or perhaps we did not even know that *is* our reality at all.

To understand and reroute a person's decisions requires that we help them to take a good look at their heart. The heart represents the centre of their world view and faith perspective, their view of God and their view of themselves. Wise choices stem from a wise heart. 'Guard your heart above all else, for it determines the course of your life' (Prov. 4:23). Discipleship of emerging adults needs to speak right into this space using the Word of God, not just worldly wisdom.

> For the word of God is alive and powerful. It is sharper than the sharpest two-edged sword, cutting between soul and spirit, between joint and marrow. It exposes our innermost thoughts and desires.
>
> *(Heb. 4:12)*

What does FOMO mean for a follower of Jesus?

In this multichoice world many face FOMO: Fear Of Missing Out. This is when somebody is scared of missing something in the (probably unjustified) impression that their friends are having a better time than they are, or making better choices. It is particularly fed by social media as people curate their newsfeeds to present themselves as having the *best* time *ever* socially, but it also applies in the world of jobs, relationships, experiences, leisure, friendships and so forth.

Because harmony, approval and relationship are such significant drivers for emerging adults, FOMO also, and rather ironically, has a flip side. This occurs when those people who genuinely are having a fantastic time are afraid of posting or even talking about the subject with those whom they know *did* miss out – so as not to offend others.

'The 'fear of missing out' is an epidemic that is stressing out us Millennials. We have a constant view to the world through the window known as Social Media, where we spend a fair amount of time refreshing the same pages looking at the highlights of other people's lives, and wondering why we're not having as much fun/wearing the right clothes/living our best lives* (*delete as appropriate). A few people will say this is ridiculous, but FOMO is real and it's not difficult to see the impact that it has. There are stats that show FOMO is now linked to anxiety, depression and alcohol misuse.'[120]

Perversely, FOMO tends to increase the likelihood of missing out either through a reluctance to commit in case a better thing comes along, or by trying to do and commit to everything – but then everything gets done half-heartedly. It might seem that FOMO is caused by having too much choice. In fact, it is more the social pressure to choose the right thing which causes genuine anxiety. It is also partly connected to how this generation is rather anaemic to living with limitations and to having to wait for outcomes. This is the Instant Generation – instant feedback and reaction is available 24/7 – instant gratification or mortification may be the results. Perhaps the greatest danger with our multichoice world is multiple distractions.

This is the contemporary environment. It is changing fast, it offers opportunity like never before, yet it can also create social anxieties and an apparent inability to take decisions of depth and long-term consequence. We must also be aware the FOMO and YOLO run the risk of paralysing people's Christian witness. They may fear nailing their colours to the mast of who they are, and what they truly believe. Wise mentors must encourage the young to 'Live clean, innocent lives as children of God, shining like bright lights in a world full of crooked and perverse people' (Phil. 2:15).

FOMO and YOLO didn't begin with the Millennials

But the wisdom from above is first of all pure. It is also peace loving, gentle at all times, and willing to yield to others. It is full of mercy and the fruit of good deeds. It shows no favouritism and is always sincere.

(James 3:17)

The root issue of FOMO lies in identity. The more secure we can help a person to feel in their true, God-ordained identity, the less likely they are to feel like they are 'missing out' in life. It's a perennial issue: Eve in the garden was tempted with FOMO, so she ate the fruit. Then Adam joined in so as not to miss out on the experience. Why? They felt they lacked something. They were insecure. It is most people's daily experience that we feel somehow bereft, insecure; we focus on what we lack rather than all we have. Humanity has been searching to fill perceived gaps since Eden. Yet the picture of Eden is one of God's abundant provision, protection, promise; 'hidden with Christ in God' (Col. 3:3) we do indeed have all we need. But we need to know it in the now.

We have such an opportunity to help emerging adults to understand that their true identity and purpose are to be found 'rooted and established in love' (Eph. 3:17, NIV), in Christ. The more a person can receive God's love for themselves, the more they may get to grips with being 'called . . . out of the darkness into his wonderful light (1 Pet. 2:9) for a God-given purpose. Then, the less they will worry about the lure of alternative choices, and the more security they will find as they discover God's choices for their life.[121]

Surrender

Let us help young adults to surrender their lives to God fully. People are reluctant to do this when they do not really trust that God has the best plan and purposes for their everyday lives. Undoubtedly, churches and families can help by fostering attitudes which focus upon the goodness and faithfulness of God. It is important that we paint a picture of our Father God who is 100 per cent *for* us. After that comes the question of obedience, which is never a popular choice, but it is a vital one.

Usually, it's a lengthy process for a person to design their life around God's values and priorities: and the ancient Holy Habits help enormously, as does patient discipleship from those who've walked the path ahead. Everything Jesus spoke about a fruitful, faithful, fearless Christian life is rooted in one thing: obedience to our Father. To know God in intimacy, to learn to hear His voice above others and then to put it into practice – this takes the sting out of FOMO, and adds the joy into discipleship. Now gaining Christ is the highest goal.

The apostle Paul acknowledged that he was good at his job, but still 'We put no confidence in human effort, though I could have confidence in my own effort if anyone could' (Phil. 3:3-4). Obedience is the key. The only FOMO Paul suffers from is gospel FOMO: 'Yes, everything else is worthless when compared with the infinite value of knowing Christ Jesus my Lord. For his sake

I have discarded everything else, counting it all as garbage, so that I could gain Christ (Phil. 3:8).

FOMO and FONSO for followers of Jesus

Over the past twenty-five years, we have observed that those young adults who prospered the most in their kingdom life were those who totally sold out to Jesus. Some kept a foot in both camps, and reaped the kind of 'lukewarm' reward of a semi-compromised Christian life. The radical ones who were willing to 'lose their life' (Matt. 16:25) in single-minded pursuit of Jesus, who were hungry for His friendship and direction, really gained a sense of purpose, passion and perseverance. Jesus made it profoundly simple: 'If you cling to your life, you will lose it, and if you let your life go, you will save it' (Luke 17:33). Perhaps we should encourage FONSO instead: 'Fear Of Not Selling Out'?

This is modern-day fear of the Lord, the very 'beginning of wisdom' (Prov. 9:10, NIV). It should also help with another common concern: fear of what others will think. This happens when our identity is derived from peer approval or acceptance. It is a feature of emerging adulthood, and it doesn't change overnight. But it does change with maturity. Let us encourage young adults to counter this inbuilt fear by living for His audience of one.

One practical method is to get them to step out and take risks which *only Jesus* can get them through. Perhaps it is prophesying or praying for healing in public, maybe it is stepping towards a godly goal that they don't yet have the money for. Short-term programmes such as discipleship years, oversees mission trips, can help because they push people out of their comfort zone, or away from the glare and power of their peers' judgements. As their maturity grows and they watch others modelling this kind of lifestyle, they will learn to generate their own 'faith gaps' for Jesus to fill. Faith is 'tested by fire', but afterwards it becomes more 'precious than gold' (1 Pet. 1:7, NKJV) because it achieves not human's approval, but God's.

It's never too early to be radical

And let us not make the mistake of thinking that young adults are somehow not ready for the most radical kind of Christian life. The kingdom call applies to all. It is always and only radical by its very definition, the greatest cause a person can sign up to. As Jesus said, it is most available to those who enter it 'like a child' in simple obedience (Matt. 18:3), secure in the knowledge that they are much-loved children of God.

Somebody's twenties or thirties is not a season of preparation to enter fully into God's purpose for their lives. The kingdom life has *already* started. It is a Western mistake to think 'they aren't ready' and must wait. In other cultures people don't get that luxury! Nick remembers being a twenty-something exploring church leadership and being humbled and challenged simply by meeting a nineteen-year-old Indonesian girl who was already leading a church plant of 700 other young adults. The earlier that somebody is required to take responsibility, the quicker they will assume it. Many heroes of our faith were very young when they radically said, 'Yes!'

What does the Bible say about YOLO?

The Bible says our purpose is to seek God through intimate relationship, and to seek the kingdom through practising Jesus' words, works and wonders. All of this is usually best done beyond the church walls, serving our cities and cultures to see them revived. We have found that certain contemporary Christian cultures have so elevated the appeal of church ministry and have put such an emphasis on finding 'my calling' or 'my purpose' or 'my ministry' in the present, that it actually works against this.

YOLO might sound like a bit of fun – 'Hey, You Only Live Once, right?' – but in fact, YOLO has a narcissistic and nihilistic root. It is self-absorbed and morally bankrupt. YOLO is essentially a mentality that says 'screw it' to life. 'It doesn't matter if I get hurt or damaged (physically or emotionally) 'cos life is short and meaningless.'

Contemporary culture may say this. Christians believe the exact opposite. Jesus' kingdom creates life and purpose – it does away with nihilism. That is why YOLO is not an attitude we should ever encourage. We prefer *carpe diem* every time. Let us inspire our emerging adults to seize the day, to make it count. Not just through an evangelistic life but in those causes like ecology and social justice that are so close the heart of these generations, because they are close to the heart of God. As the apostle Peter says, 'Now we live with great expectation' (1 Pet. 1:3)

The big danger with YOLO and FOMO is to think, 'What am I doing wrong?' Emerging adulthood is a season when one's identity is forged and solidified. It is crucial that those discipling keep the focus upon how the Father sees His beloved children, commanding and empowering them to live from this identity. Instead, because of Jesus we can ask the question, 'What am I doing right?' Rooted in faith, not fear, not searching for love, security and approval in less satisfying places. Jesus has raised us *out* of the lifestyle of fear and FOMO.

Since you have been raised to new life with Christ, set your sights on the realities of heaven, where Christ sits in the place of honour at God's right hand. Think about the things of heaven, not the things of earth. For you died to this life, and your real life is hidden with Christ in God.

(Col. 3:1-3)

110. Get a Life by Soul II Soul, 1996. Written by: John Everett Ott, Samuel Robert Rivers, Wesley Louden Borland, William Frederick Durst. Lyrics © Universal Music Publishing Group https://www.lyrics.com/lyric/1645406/The+Number+One+Rap+Album/Get+a+Life.
111. Kelly Clarkson, *Meaning of Life*, 2017 Composed by James Morrison Catchpole, Ilsey Juber, Jesse Shatkin © Atlantic Records.
112. Richard Dunn and Jana L. Sundene, *Shaping the Journey of Emerging Adults* (Downers Grove, IL: IVP, 2012) p. 25. Edited.
113. Christian Smith and Patricia Snell, *Souls in Transition: The Religious & Spiritual Lives of Emerging Adults* (New York: Oxford University Press, 2009), p. 6.
114. Aamna Mohdin, 'Nearly a Million More Young Adults Now Live with Parents – Study', *The Guardian*, Guardian News and Media, 8 February 2019, www.theguardian.com/society/2019/feb/08/million-more-young-adults-live-parents-uk-housing (accessed 6.12.19).
115. Management and leadership theory, first coined in 1987 but just as pertinent to the global situation and the kind of atmosphere and politics our young adults grow up in today.
116. Sitara Kurian, *Meet the Millennials* (London: KPMG LLP, 2017), p. 11, https://home.kpmg/content/dam/kpmg/uk/pdf/2017/04/Meet-the-Millennials-Secured.pdf (accessed 5.12.19) shows that in 2010 UK male graduates worked in an average of three companies within the first five years after graduation.
117. Claire Madden, 'Move over Millennials: Everything to Know about Gen Z', Vogue Australia, 24 November 2019, www.vogue.com.au/culture/features/move-over-millennials-everything-to-know-about-gen-z/news-story/2ddef9cb4ff31b7b4934454a002676cf (accessed 5.12.19).
118. Forge Leadership Consultancy, *Millennial Leaders: Now is Our Time and this is Our Voice* (London: Forge Leadership Consultancy, 2018), p. 9.
119. Ibid. See endnote 116.
120. Rob Chivers, 'The Fear of Missing Out', blog post on Student Christian Movement website 7 December 2017 www.movement.org.uk/blog/fear-missing-out (accessed 6.12.19).
121. This is what we believe to be the correct understanding and experience of the famously encouraging psalm 'Take delight in the LORD, and he will give you your heart's desires' (Ps. 37:4). It is not that God fulfils all your desires, it is the other way around! As you delight in Him, His desires become your desires.

CHAPTER FIFTEEN

Intolerant Tolerance

I disapprove of what you say, but I will defend to the death your right to say it.

Voltaire[122]

Young adults celebrate diversity and tolerance as one of their key contributions to contemporary culture. Perhaps more than any past generation, today's will champion the rights of those on the edge and are generally accepting of a multiplicity of lifestyles and views. They simply will not recognise a person's difference as any reason to think less of them or to discriminate. Much of what previous generations held as socially inappropriate is simply a non-issue for today's generation. This applies just as much to young adults within our churches. Emerging culture *does* really care about discrimination, inclusion, social justice, and they will fight for what they believe in. This is the kingdom of God coming close to earth.

For those people in their twenties that have stuck with church since childhood, a Church of England survey has shown that tolerance was a very significant factor: 'the most important attribute of a church should be that it is "friendly" and "non-judgemental".'[123] It is encouraging that young adult Christians we know will focus upon unity, asking, 'What do we have in common?' and will become really uncomfortable and perhaps disturbed by conflict between Christians, as being a bad witness. They will gather together regardless of traditional church/denominational boundaries. In our city we have appreciated worship gatherings organised by university students where Christians from all variety of churches attend without thinking twice about what kind of theology might be represented. They look for unity and togetherness; they are far less bothered by the old divides and categories. Certainly they are far less interested or even aware of denominations. Nor are they keen to be part of any particular church's 'empire building'.

How tolerant are we really?

Britain has prided itself since the Second World War as being a tolerant nation, welcoming multiculturalism and teaching the principle of inclusion in our schools. Tolerance may be defined as a form of *acceptance*, as the 'willingness to accept behaviour and beliefs that are different from your own, although you might not agree with or approve of them' and also a *capacity to cope*: 'the ability to deal with something unpleasant or annoying, or to continue existing despite bad or difficult conditions'.[124]

But how tolerant is our current culture really?

Attitudes have shifted rapidly in the past ten years. Now it is often *not* OK to hold views which others strongly disapprove of. In some instances society will no longer defend your right to hold such views. As postmodernity takes hold, society is becoming inconsistent, even irrational, in how we apply our tolerance and inclusion to those with alternative views.

Our present age is not as unique and progressive as it believes. Those most supportive of free expression are often least supportive of freedom of conscience or free speech which disagrees with their viewpoint. The danger is that this kind of thinking is also increasingly being applied towards the tenets of our orthodox Christian faith.

Think of the widespread response in Westernised nations to the attacking of French satirical magazine *Charlie Hebdo* in

January 2015. Islamic terrorists killed journalists for publishing cartoon portrayals of the prophet Mohammed, whose depiction some branches of Islam outlaw. The magazine was infamous for its stridently secularist, left-wing satire, frequently mocking all of the world's major religions. The world rose up to defend the right to free speech – millions changed their Facebook profile picture to a French flag – moral outrage ensued. Yet in 2019, Facebook was widely acclaimed for banning various hard-right political parties from having a platform to espouse their views. British Labour MP Yvette Cooper, as chair of the influential Home Affairs Select Committee said, 'All companies need to be accountable for the material they host or publish and take some responsibility. We all know the appalling consequences there can be if hateful, violent and illegal content is allowed to proliferate.'[125] In four years, publishing platforms have been pressurised to eradicate content which inspires hate or bigotry, and free speech is no longer the clarion call.

Another example is the practice of university unions and societies 'no-platforming' visiting speakers. This is when an invited speaker is objected to, usually by small-scale special interest groups, on the grounds that their views are offensive. Pressure is applied either to shout them down or to have them banned from campus in advance. In the UK, all sorts of people have been targeted or banned in recent years, from Brexit talisman Nigel Farage to the legendary women's rights campaigner Germaine Greer. Recent analysis found that 90 per cent of UK universities are restrictive of free speech. In 2019 the UK government moved to end 'no-platforming' because of issues of free speech, but its practice has been defended by the National Union of Students deputy president saying,

'Students' unions are often the only place where students can be themselves, a place where they can think about things and challenge ideas and thoughts in a safe environment. Sometimes the only way you can ensure those safe spaces remain safe is through no-platform policies.'[126]

Intolerant tolerance

What is really happening is intolerant tolerance.

There is an incoherent distinction made in practice between tolerance and inclusion. Today, the situation is not just 'we tolerate', it is more 'we celebrate' certain kinds of diversity. Yet the twist in the tail is that people are far less tolerant of attitudes and behaviours they simply do not like or agree with. If toleration may broadly be defined as 'you put up with what you don't like', then society has stopped being tolerant, despite its rhetoric.

Help me to find my compass bearings

In a postmodern culture where much of society's inherited frameworks such as family are being deconstructed, it is vital that we help young Christians to find their biblical compass bearings. The discipleship challenge for today is to help and equip our emerging generations to navigate this moral maze. As Simon Barrington says, 'whereas baby boomers want to get out of the maze, millennials want to live in the maze well.'[127]

This means churches still need to do the hard work of building for people a coherent ethical biblical framework, grounded in the example of Jesus – otherwise there is no foundation from which to build a structure of meaning, of values, of choices in how to live well. At The Well Sheffield, even within the same community groups we regularly find that people hold polarised views on contentious issues such as politics, same-sex relationships and so forth. It is important that we maintain a culture in which we genuinely love and respect one another, learn to listen to one another, and model ourselves on the famous Berean people in Acts 17 who were open-minded enough to search the Scriptures to test for the truth when they encountered alternative ideas.

Tolerance or transformation?

Tolerance is important, but Christianity is about transformation, not simply tolerance. Jesus has low tolerance for deliberate sin, but such a high tolerance of the person's soul that He provides a way through, a way to a better kind of 'life in all its fulness' (John 10:10, GNT) through life in the Spirit. Jesus' teaching is clear and uncompromising. Come as you are, but do not expect to stay as you are. 'Come, follow me . . .'

Jesus said He comes to shine light into situations and people: 'I am the light of the world. If you follow me, you won't have to walk in darkness, because you will have the light that leads to life.' (John 8:12). This assumes there is darkness, and a need for renewal. To Nicodemus He says: 'I tell you the truth, unless you are born again, you cannot see the Kingdom of God' (John 3:3). In other words, you'll stay blind and in darkness until you fully submit your life to Mine. To His disciples: 'If any of you wants to be my follower, you must give up your own way, take up your cross, and follow me' (Matt. 16:24). To a woman caught in adultery He says: 'I do not condemn you either. Go. From now on sin no more' (John 8:11, AMP).

To anybody who wants to be His disciple, He still says 'Come follow me.'[128]

John Wesley Reid summarises this brilliantly:

Tolerance flies in the face of the gospel because it is apathetic both to brokenness and holiness, and when we don't recognize our brokenness then we will never recognize our need for holiness . . . and thus Jesus becomes, at best, superfluous . . . But the problem with tolerance is that when we accept people for who they WANT to be, we neglect the people that Jesus MADE them to be . . . The gospel does not boast 'come as you are, stay as you are' but rather 'come as you are TO BE RESTORED!'[129]

Did Jesus differentiate between people? Yes: on the basis of His benchmark obedience to the kingdom. He formed a select small group of devotees and confidants. He excluded most Pharisees and told some people that the kind of righteousness the Pharisees pursued would exclude them from inheriting the kingdom (Matt. 5:20). Yet, He was surprisingly and radically inclusive towards those whom society consider to be outcasts. *Why?* Because they were 'poor in spirit', meaning they recognised their need of God. Those are the ones He calls blessed (Matt. 5:3, NIV). That is the kind of humble raw material that God loves to work with.

The Church's response

There is a very important call on today's Church in public to resolve our differences well and in love, so that an outside world is clear what we are in favour of, rather than just what we are against. There is so much opportunity for the national Church to be positive, cause-driven, to be seen to be seeking to improve the world. That is the zeitgeist of this generation.

The Church, however, is in the world but not of it. A time has come when the norms of our prevailing culture have moved so far from a Christian perspective that the Church needs, at appropriate times and in appropriate ways, clearly to take a stand and voice the values of our orthodox faith. This takes wisdom, courage and discernment, since our aim is never to cause division but to speak up for what we believe is right in God's sight. This is not just for the sake of taking a public stance, but for the everyday discipleship of our members. If they hear nothing to the contrary, they will simply imbibe what society presents.

In 2018 the nation of Ireland held an historic referendum on legalising abortion, which was banned in most cases due to the nation's strong Catholic heritage. We spoke with some of our church leader friends in the capital Dublin who all shared how shocked they were by how much their young people's opinions on the subject were shaped by the secular news media and by the loudest voices in culture. Even though they did not normally talk about politics from the pulpit, some churches filled with young adults found that this referendum had become not just a political issue but a discipleship issue. No matter where people were coming from in the spectrum of opinion the principal aim for church leaders was to help their congregations to make a balanced, biblical judgement on the issues at hand. In the end, they did not all vote in the same way but at least they had given some careful, Christian consideration to the issues.

Discipleship is about helping people to catch such a glorious vision of Jesus in His resurrection power that they fall in love with everything about God. It is about facilitating people to choose to follow Jesus' words, works, ways and wonders. It is about obedience to a kingdom of God world view, and a holy life. All done in the certain hope that nobody stays still in the kingdom. We walk and sometimes stumble into a transformation of heart and soul, which is not only good for us, it is for the benefit of society and creation itself.[130] To follow Jesus is to change to become more like Him.

Case Study:

Josh (age twenty-nine)

In March 2019 I'd finally hit rock bottom. Life wasn't working anymore and nothing I tried seemed to fill the giant void I felt inside myself. I was suffering with anxiety and depression and on three separate occasions had tried, yet thankfully failed, to take my own life. My drinking was out of control and I'd begun to use drugs as a means of escape. I was chasing relationship after relationship believing casual sex would make me feel alive. None of it lasts though, it's momentary and as soon as the high was over I was back to rock bottom looking for my next fix in any form I could find.

Life this way wasn't living but merely surviving, and my will to carry on was gone. I had to make a change! I chose to give my life to Jesus at The Well Sheffield after an encounter with the Holy Spirit in a way that words cannot describe, but I can hand on heart say is the best decision I've ever made. I'm now free from addiction and filled with hope for my future. Days are meaningful and peace fills me each morning. Faith doesn't make it easy, but it does make it possible.

122. This quote may be attributed to Voltaire, passed on via the historian Evelyn Beatrice Hall in 1906, in reference to the attitudes of Voltaire in the late eighteenth century. 'I Disapprove of What You Say', *Quote Investigator*, 12 October 2019, www.quoteinvestigator.com/2015/06/01/defend-say/ (accessed 5.12.19).
123. Church of England Education Office, *Rooted in the Church: Summary Report November 2016* (London: 2016), p. 3, https://www.churchofengland.org/sites/default/files/2017-10/2016_rooted_in_the_church_summary_report.pdf (accessed 5.12.19).
124. 'Tolerance', Cambridge Dictionary, ©Cambridge University Press, 2019 dictionary.cambridge.org/dictionary/english/tolerance (accessed 5.12.19).
125. Alex Hern, 'Facebook Bans Far-Right Groups', *The Guardian*, Guardian News and Media, 18 April 2019, www.theguardian.com/technology/2019/apr/18/facebook-bans-far-right-groups-including-bnp-edl-and-britain-first (accessed 5.12.19).
126. Ross Logan, '"Accept a Debate" Universities to Be FINED If Student Unions Ban Controversial Speakers', Express.co.uk, 19 October 2017, www.express.co.uk/news/uk/868700/free-speech-no-platform-universities-fined-students-union-ban-speakers-jo-johnson (accessed 5.12.19).
127. Abi Jarvis, 'Millennial Leadership', Evangelical Alliance, 18 October 2018, www.eauk.org/news-and-views/millenial-leadership (accessed 5.12.19).
128. For example, Matthew 4:19; Matthew 19:21; Mark 1:17; Mark 10:21; Luke 9:59.
129. John Wesley Reid, '5 Trends Christian Millennials MUST STOP Doing', johnwesleyreid.com, 17 August 2018, www.johnwesleyreid.com/post/5-trends-christian-millennials-must-stop-doing (accessed 5.12.19).
130. Romans 8:22-24.

SECTION FOUR

Our Response

For the Mighty One is holy,
and he has done great things for me.
He shows mercy from generation to generation
to all who fear him.
His mighty arm has done tremendous things!
He has scattered the proud and haughty ones.
He has brought down princes from their thrones
and exalted the humble.
He has filled the hungry with good things
and sent the rich away with empty hands.
He has helped his servant Israel
and remembered to be merciful.
For he made this promise to our ancestors,
to Abraham and his children forever.

Luke 1:49-55

CHAPTER SIXTEEN

Snowflakes or Avalanches?

'you are not special, you are not a beautiful and unique snowflake'

(Chuck Palahniuk, Fight Club)[131]

Western Millennials are sometimes stereotyped as 'snowflakes'. The term is generally used pejoratively to describe a group of entitled, politically correct, militant, selfie-taking, flighty, emotionally vulnerable souls with no grip on the real world.

Broadly, this is a mistake. In the midst of some real challenges and some quirky characteristics, a generation is rising up who are fed up with the status quo and the political climate. They have witnessed what a lack of faith and spirituality has done to their parents' generation. They really care about the world around them and the world they will leave behind, and they are making small but very significant and highly creative steps to be and find solutions to problems. They are surprising us with their bold actions and they may indeed leave behind significant societal changes. It is driven by a determination, resourcefulness and resilience which belies the challenges they face.

In 2018-19, while Europe's politicians and public were caught up in Brexit, a young lady appeared from nowhere mobilising people of every generation and challenging those who held the current positions of power to think beyond themselves and to take action against climate change. Whether you love or loathe her, at just sixteen years old, Greta Thunberg birthed an international youth movement as her strike in front of the Swedish Parliament inspired youngsters from all around the world to walk out of school and take to the streets, calling for rapid change in our politics and personal lifestyles. This wasn't the first time in history the crowds took to the streets to protest against an out-of-touch political and social power, but it is the first time a young teenager sparked an international movement.

Meet Generation Z. A generation that does actually believe that one person can make a difference. They believe they can make their mark on the world precisely because of their understanding of being unique. Millennials will be remembered for their love of brand clothing. Generation Z are busy creating their own personalised brands. This generation isn't waiting for permission; they are getting on with doing things differently and often behind the scenes. Greatly angered by the male and stale politicians, this generation is rising up as powerful, not powerless. Greta Thunberg found an unexpected global stage but most of the campaigning and cumulative action occurs at a local community level. There is a generation emerging who refuse to succumb to inertia.

'I'm not afraid of risks, will you take a risk on me?'

It has been really fun for us Gen-Xers to observe the rise of the 'Hipsters' – arguably the most original, artistic subculture for decades. Whether it has been the innovative way they can regenerate a dilapidated terrace house in our city, the care with which they can pour me a cup of coffee, or the ingenuity that fuels social media design, we can only marvel at their creativity. Generation Z are now taking this creativity and entrepreneurialism further. Recently we chatted to a speech therapist in her twenties who explained that she actually had two jobs: her medical day job and her online clothes sales business. She marketed her products through her personal social media networks in common with many of her peers who are ambitious to be 'financially independent' in just a few years.

Like yeast in the dough, entrepreneurialism runs through the veins of Generations Y and Z. This will do wonders for kingdom initiatives if we let it loose. The question is, will our churches or kingdom initiatives take the risk and pass over the reins to these generations now? The fruitfulness of any organisation (or church) is dependent upon the degree to which we recognise the talents and giftings in those around us and empower these individuals to reach their full potential. Our emerging generations have an ability to think outside the box, whether it comes to solutions to problems in a business, dealing with the homeless of the city, or communicating in public. They are a risk-taking generation who attempt small hidden initiatives, fuelled by big thinking. They are not afraid of risks.

The vital question for the Church of today is, how much are we taking a risk on them?

Please take the time to ask yourself these kinds of questions:

Are we creating a culture in which young adults can dream and start something new?

Are we allowing them to influence our programmes, strategy, governance, communication, evangelistic initiatives?

Case Study:

Unlikely candidates

My (Marjorie) first experience of church planting was in 1992 in Dublin. I had just become a disciple and joined a small team planting a new church into an old building in the centre of the city. I was the only student on the team, and to my surprise the pastor asked me to lead the student ministry. I felt very honoured and was excited about the potential vision to reach my peers, but I laugh when I look back because I see that he did not have any other options! But he could see that I was leadership material and his challenge to step up brought the best out in me.

Beginning new initiatives always creates new opportunities for new people.

Then our pastor surprised people by involving a local lad called Eoghan to play the drums. He wasn't a Christian yet, he was a bit rough around the edges, but he was an excellent drummer. He did not look like the right 'fit' for church. He responded to being loved, welcomed and invited into a family on a mission. Drawing him into the worship team and using his natural abilities meant that he was in the right place to encounter God's transforming Spirit. Not long later he also became a young adult leader and a disciple of Jesus.

I love the fact that I have been leading young adults and students ever since and Eoghan is now the senior pastor of that same church. It is amazing what can happen when we take risks on people, and look to their destiny rather than their present or past.

Release me to dream for myself

In the UK today we see a few great examples of churches led by and shaped by Millennial leaders. It is not necessary that every church leader over the age of fifty must suddenly resign in favour of young blood! But if we are serious about reaching, raising and releasing the rising generations, we must be intentional in doing so. In Sheffield we have found it helpful to deliberately create opportunities to release younger volunteers and leaders: even when that feels too early or a bit unwise. What keeps it safe is a culture of high support.

People become what we call them to. If you do not know where to start on this one, we would encourage you to create a permission-giving culture where people know they can dream and be heard. As leaders, we can often mistakenly feel like we have to come up with all the dreams and ideas. That is exhausting for us and disempowering for others, but many churches operate like this. Generations Y and Z have many new dreams to birth. Let us empower our rising adults by reminding them of God's old and big story and the cause of which they are a part. Let us inspire them as to the past and believe in them for the future.

Case Study:
Dreaming with God

When we launched The Well Sheffield in 2015 we preached for the inaugural year on two topics: the kingdom of God, and dreaming with God. Alongside some existing disciples, we quickly began to gather new Christians and many 'de-churched' who felt safe and ready to return to Christian community after perhaps ten to fifteen years of feeling isolated or rejected by organised Church. It was a beautiful time. It was a season for God to restore some people's old dreams and prophetic promises, and we were confident that He would sow new vision and purpose into those coming to faith.

Permission-giving is a very powerful force in the local church; however, Nick soon observed that people needed help to turn their God-given dreams into something tangible. So he designed a short five-session course to do just that. We called it: 'Dreams to Reality: How to start new initiatives inspired by God.' Topics included how to get godly vision and passions; what does kingdom mission look like; understanding our culture and context; limitations/understanding ourselves; kingdom leadership in the workplace; team leading; the dynamics of a start-up – all peppered with lots of practical case studies by local Christian entrepreneurs, local social enterprise founders, and life coaches. Each time we have run the course it has been incredibly encouraging to witness people clarify their dreams and come away with a plan of action. For example, it helped one Millennial girl to shape her passion for the elderly into an award-winning dementia care and awareness programme. It has now birthed several new outreach ministries through The Well.

A healthy support structure

As we create a culture in which the young and inexperienced are released, it is important that we also offer high levels of support. Individual snowflakes are precious but fragile.

When we chat with the young dreamers and leaders in our midst, they are not necessarily afraid of failure, but they become the most confident to step out and try new things where there is a good support network around them. They are not looking for the churches and environments with the biggest show or stage. They will be drawn to people and places where it is safe to take risks and fail, where people believe in them. Churches can best enable this by fostering a culture which is rooted in our strong identity in Christ, where you can have a good go and even fail, but you are never seen as a failure.

Let's be honest. If we are to create a dreaming, risk-taking culture, then most leaders will have to actively resist the temptation to micromanage others. We will need to switch from asking people to do what we think needs to be done, towards helping people discover their own dreams, callings and expressions of God's kingdom in action. For some local churches, this may mean a difficult but crucial culture shift.

We were asked by a church minister whether this 'dreaming culture' feels rather chaotic and a haphazard way of coming up with vision. Quite the opposite. We see it as a key function of apostolic leadership whereby local church pastors set the framework and culture, vision and values, but always seek to empower people to express themselves within it. It is not an absence of leadership. The church leader still has the role to help identify and call out the gold in people, spot when they may not have seen it themselves, channelling people and resource behind new initiatives as they emerge.

What makes snowflakes unique

Let us make human beings in our image . . .

(Genesis 1:26)

You are unique! We all are. But it is essential that we live knowing where our true value comes from. For all the criticism, Generation Y's understanding of their own uniqueness should be viewed as hugely positive. The Christian biblical framework for life establishes that every human being is uniquely and creatively made in the image of God. If the emerging generations carry a sense of their own value, then imagine the power of connecting them to their identity as children of God.

If you are 'in Christ', your divine value lies in the fact that you are part of the most beautiful family of all time and you are a precious individual with enormous potential (1 Cor. 12:12-13; 2 Cor. 5:17). A living stone in the temple of Christ; a vital part of His body on earth, the Church (1 Pet. 2:5; 1 Cor. 12:27). It is the most important secret of the universe. When humans freeze water . . . we get ice cubes. If God freezes water . . . we get individual snowflakes, moulded by the chemistry of community. He has His handprint on each one of us.

Take time to love me well ... but don't fake it

One only has to take a look across today's workplace culture to see some of the changes taking place in leadership style now that Millennials are becoming the majority. Workplace cultures have increasingly high levels of feedback, encouragement and creative vision. From secondary school upwards, young people are being taught to dream in teams and work in collaboration.

Sadly, traditional patterns of local church leadership or governance have a long way to catch up. Often, despite its rhetoric, the Church can be hugely hierarchically driven – a select senior few come up with the ideas and everyone else is expected to implement them. We probably need to listen more carefully. For the younger leaders around us, relationship trumps task and achievement. They look for real relationship, not tokenism or line management. Do not allow a well-crafted organisational structure with staff meetings and even 'discipleship groups' deceive you. This is the generation that craves authenticity. They recognise quite quickly if you actually care about them and believe in them.

We recently interviewed for the role of youth minister in our church. We allowed the youth to be part of this process, a collaborative model now found in many secondary school appointments. One of the questions the youth put forward to the candidate amused us, but is so pertinent: 'Do you actually like us?'

There's more to me than meets the eye ... let's work together

Many have commented that this generation longs for fulfilling work. Today's young people want their everyday jobs to make a difference to society and resolve societal issues. Fuelled by their entrepreneurial attitude, they are tearing up the old hymn sheet. According to a study commissioned by Solopress, more than half the UK university students (56 per cent) are considering setting up their own business.[132] The desire for meaningful work means that young professionals today are willing to take up less well-paid positions if the job creates a greater sense of satisfaction.

We are all made for meaningful work, expressed since the Garden of Eden, and this generation's approach to kingdom work will be no different. Today's younger generations are the most financially challenged individuals for decades; yet they are seemingly the most resourceful. But it is clear that to see these passions succeed will require the older generations investing differently, listening to dreams and being similarly fuelled to want to construct a world that is fair, just and compassionate.

It is here that we think the Western Church has such an opportunity.

The Church is the one trusted community where different generations mix together in committed relationships with a common cause. What would happen if a full spectrum of resources released from the spectrum of ages were allowed to rub shoulders? The creative thinking of the young coupled with financial investment of the older could catalyse an explosion of kingdom action.

At no time in history has there been such a convergence in society where science, politics and business are coming together on certain subjects. Let us make sure we as the Church are operating in the same vein, coming together as a diverse people-group and working with other community groups and churches for the sake of the city, the region and the people around us. If we can achieve this kind of cohesion, then our snowflakes will begin to form avalanches!

They are beautiful and unique, but in large numbers they may become an unstoppable avalanche that will bury you.

(Chuck Palahniuk, Fight Club)[133]

Changing times

Traditional trajectories are breaking down. If fewer students want to work for the faceless corporate companies, even fewer want to buy their products. Almost half of people surveyed by brand agency Amplify in 2016 (45 per cent) said they would refuse to buy a product from a company that had an ethos they disagreed with.[134] It is now cool to care. Consumers are asking more questions than ever before; they want to know where their food is from, who made their clothes and who was potentially damaged in the process.

We are filled with hope that if we support these rising generations, we now stand at a point in history where systemic cancers such as global inequality could actually be rectified. The kind of changes we long for in the developing world will only come as Western nations are discipled into changing their ways in compassion and collaboration.

With our heads down in the present, we easily forget how fast things can change, and how quickly a change that starts on the fringe can escalate into a tipping point. Just look at the sudden momentum to reduce plastics waste. In 2015, mainstream society did not seem too concerned about single-use plastics. Plastic bags were freely used in supermarkets and shops. The next four years saw a large-scale revolt against single use plastics. Britain has now committed to a twenty-five-year plan that will phase out disposable packaging by 2042.[135] What winds of change are beginning to blow in your social, city or church context?

It is easy to become so comfortable or even overwhelmed by the weight of the status quo that we fail to spot the seeds of change springing up in our midst. Let us not take our eyes off these seeds, because they may well represent the kingdom of God springing up in our midst (Matt. 13:1-23).

But in an age where it is very popular to passionately take up 'ethical causes', it is important to be clear with disciples that true fulfilment is found as we discern His will for us and take up His cause. We cannot be defined only by human need or brokenness, or our part to play will be short-lived. Nor can we be defined by popular thinking, or the latest trends.

We are instead a people marked out by the presence of God, and our behaviour is to be representative of that of our Saviour: servant leadership. The cross was His cause. His Father unveiled the plan and Jesus walked in total obedience to His Father and in so doing, laid down His life for His people. As we come to understand God's will and act upon it, we will change the world for the better.

Take up His cause not our own

Our identity as children of God laid out in the opening chapters of Genesis is two-fold: to be with God and to work for God. Our personal journey of faith has been to receive the radical grace of first concentrating on being with God, as much-loved children. But it doesn't stop there. It's not all or only about the 'being'. This is only half of the picture. The doing – the work we have to do on God's behalf – is just as much part of the equation. In Genesis 1 God said humanity was made to 'rule' (Gen. 1:26, NIV) and this purpose is core to who we are.

'By me kings reign' says Proverbs 8:15.[136] Years later, in the Gospels Jesus outlines that His rule and reign are 'at hand'[137] and the invitation for every follower of His is to learn to partner and to rule with Him. If we have a true sense of our identity as sons and daughters, we will be able to take up the causes on our Father's heart, and welcome the shift in our own priorities. After all, Jesus said that He did 'only what he [saw] the Father doing' (John 5:19).

Case Study:

Testimony time!

Our culture at The Well Sheffield is to put a huge emphasis on testimony; that is, storytelling and thanksgiving as to how

God is moving amid the highs and lows of our everyday lives. We hear stories at almost every service; stories of people who have recently encountered God; of personal transformation; of serving our city; of people stepping out in their identity as missionaries reaching others.

Undoubtedly this fuels positive thinking and opens up the door for God to move through individuals who hear and respond in faith. We are always struck by the extraordinary potential that resides within ordinary individuals walking close to Almighty God. We are reminded that followers of Christ filled with the power and presence of God are pretty much unstoppable. They are captivated by the cause of His kingdom. They are caught up in a movement that began 2,000 years. It is an old story, a wonderfully big story we find ourselves in the middle of, and a story that has new chapters being drafted all the time. God's transforming power is immense in every generation.

One story becomes a catalyst for another, and together we write the big story.

There is an invitation for us to take up our cross and set out on this incredible kingdom adventure for our heavenly Dad. His cause is an eternal one. His kingdom is broad and He may lead you to people and places you would never have dreamt of. Together, we really can change the world for the better. Let the avalanche begin!

131. Chuck Palahniuk, *Fight Club: A Novel* (New York: W.W. Norton, 1st edition, 1996).
132. Solopress Ltd., 'Modern Student Business: The New Student Worker' (Southend-on-Sea, 2018), https://www.solopress.com/blog/wp-content/uploads/2018/04/Final-Solopress-whitepaper1.pdf (accessed 5.12.19).
133. Ibid. See endnote 131.
134. Amplify, London, 2016. *Young Blood. Exploring modern youth culture.* https://www.weareamplify.com/young-blood/ (accessed 12.2.20).
135. Joe Watts, 'Theresa May Vows to Eliminate UK's Plastic Waste by 204.,' *The Independent*, Independent Digital News and Media, 11 January 2018, www.independent.co.uk/news/uk/politics/plastic-waste-uk-theresa-may-2042-vow-commitment-a8152446.html (accessed 6.12.19).
136. NIV.
137. For example, Matthew 3:2, ESV.

CHAPTER SEVENTEEN

The Church of the Future

In April 2019 in the run-up to a heated leadership contest which eventually saw Boris Johnson become British Prime Minister, the incumbent Health Secretary Matt Hancock wrote a short newspaper article listing three reasons why Millennials are put off from voting for the Conservative Party.[138] If it was instructive for them, it most certainly rings a bell for the British church today:

1. Talking/pointing out problems not solutions

2. Harking back to the past and past glories

3. Miscommunicating and misapplying their values so that Millennials don't see the connections between Conservative values and Millennial values.

Mr Hancock was frustrated because he felt his party had values and solutions of worth which the emerging generations ought to connect with — if only his own side could get smarter at bridging the communications gap, speaking their language, connecting long-held principles with contemporary culture.

Does this sound familiar?

Today's public marketplace of ideas or entertainment is crowded, many loud and appealing voices compete for attention. Sometimes the Church in the West feels small and misunderstood, a remnant of God's faithful people. We *know* that we carry the message which transforms nations and sets individuals into fullness of life. Yet it feels like we are swimming against the tide, shouting into the wind.

Can we find ways to explain the 'why' of Christianity to today's generations?

Discipleship first

In January 2017 a new leader with a clear vision for his people stepped forward at his inauguration ceremony in front of a worldwide audience, and boldly proclaimed:

> From this day forward, a new vision will govern our land. From this moment on, it's going to be America First. America First.

And a few moments later the new President Trump said things which the Millennials in his audience could have written themselves:

> In America, we understand that a nation is only living as long as it is striving. We will no longer accept politicians who are all talk and no action – constantly complaining but never doing anything about it. The time for empty talk is over. Now arrives the hour of action.[139]

We are not for one minute suggesting that our churches should be modelled on Donald Trump's leadership, but to his credit, he has always been crystal clear on his top priorities. What could this sound like for the Church today?

Discipleship first.

The need is not really for bigger churches, but bigger Christians. Those who live with an understanding of what it means to be 'in Christ'. Our nation's church leaders and practising Christians face a stark choice: to manage our existing decline in attendance and influence, or to do something different and radical – like Jesus did – in order to reboot our faithful remnant, and to establish those coming in new to Christianity on firm foundations. To generate a body of believers who live as sold-out missionary disciples of their glorious King Jesus, and the principles of the kingdom of God. Two thousand years ago Jesus messed with His society's prevailing concepts of what true religion looked like, creating instead a movement of empowered, interconnected disciples. Today that movement carries the potential to transform any society, anywhere, within a generation.

Will we be willing to do or design church to achieve the outcomes which Jesus laid out in his Gospels? And to do so in a countercultural way that forms genuine apprentices or disciples of Jesus, rather than forming consumers of contemporary culture or Church culture? People who take responsibility for asking themselves 'What is God saying?' and 'What am I going to do about it?' and looking to replicate themselves and their discipleship into the lives of others?

An agenda for spiritual awakening

> And I will make a covenant of peace with them, an everlasting covenant. I will give them their land and increase their numbers, and I will put my Temple among them forever. I will make my home among them. I will be their God, and they will be my people.
>
> *(Ezek. 37:26-27)*

If we are to see an authentic expression of the Christian life within current culture, then a white-hot centre at the heart of our lives and churches is absolutely crucial. The more secular society becomes, the more there is a need for raw Holy Spirit breakout. Personally, we decided years ago that we did not want simply to be ministers in a church, but to be revivalists of the generations. We live in the expectancy that there is always more of God available to us; that union with Christ can be an ever-deepening reality for us, and that the world around us is in desperate need of His resurrection power. While we long and pray for a powerful move of God in our time we can all choose to be revivalists today!

This only happens when we are intentional. We always have an eye on the spiritual temperature of our local church, always ready to make adjustments. For example, over the last few years we have discerned God asking us to lengthen our times of corporate worship, to offer healing prayer to the public, to take more risks in sharing the gospel beyond our building's walls and to give some of our budget away to bless other churches. Above everything comes the call to prayer. To pray for our nation and generation requires perseverance. We have found that it really helps to set rhythms of prayer which are easy to remember and get involved with, on a daily and monthly basis.

Meaningful measurements

We encourage all those within church to consider the 'why' and 'how' of reaching, raising and releasing Generations Y and Z to flourish as missionary disciples in today's world. That means designing a culture which fosters church visions, values and structures aimed at:

- Understanding them
- Empowering them: not just into leadership and mission, but in their own exploration of spirituality and discipleship
- Releasing the next generation to dream a kingdom dream, and have a good go
- Powerful encounters in the presence of God

- Having them in leadership, and being willing to be led by them

- Helping them to process life's struggles, battles, demons. Building scaffolding around them so they may not just acknowledge their baggage, but be willing to address it deeply, and feel safe enough to journey towards emotional health and wholeness

- Mentoring them among the multigenerational connections which the Church uniquely offers to society

- Connecting their generation's passion for social change and justice to the Church's historic mission

Changing Church: What needs to go, what needs to stay?

We need to be courageous enough to challenge and change our existing models, methods and measurements. To be careful how we define our measurements of health, success, or even growth. Success is not about how many young adults are attending church. Success is more about how many young adults are attending upon Jesus in personal, passionate devotion to His presence which overflows. As the saying goes, let us measure success not by our seating capacity, but by our sending capacity.

The rest of this chapter makes the following recommendations for change in more detail:

- Restructure church leadership to include young adults at every level

- Developing pathways which raise radical disciples and support young adults during times of transition

- Presenting church in ways that help, not hinder

- Ensuring the church shapes and speaks into culture, not the other way around

What practical steps can the local church take to enable these shifts?

Have young adults as elders and board members

One answer would be to diversify our own local church leadership teams – so that they are not all white, British, male, fifty-plus dominated. Yes, this is a sweeping stereotype, and we are not seeking to cause offence. But positive shifts in that direction would speak volumes to an emerging culture which so values diversity and inclusion. Be honest for a moment and consider who really shapes your church community, and who has the least effective voice at present. Up and down our nation the young generations are largely absent from positions of genuine influence within our churches and denominations/movements.

We propose that diversity in the local church is not just about structural leadership. It must also include who is represented on the stage/pulpit, in publicity, on the website, in the congregational decision-making forums and so forth. Not token representation – actual representation, with a voice and input that is honoured. Remember, young adults who value authenticity will see straight through anything else. A recent Church of England report asked what helps to keep young people rooted in the worshipping life of the local church into their adult years. One key conclusion was a desire for inclusion in leadership and decisions.

'Young people seek to be treated as equal members of the Church. They want to have meaningful roles, not tokenism. This includes leadership roles and serving opportunities, including intergenerational ministry. They also seek a greater 'voice and vote' on decision-making bodies such as PCCs and Synods.'[140]

We have to ask ourselves why we would *not* actively promote diversity in our local church leadership and public presentation?

Almost every church is multi-age and multicultural: that is the beauty of church. In some congregations there may not be many younger people, but let us begin by trusting those younger people we do have. Valuing them, honouring God's work in them – even though it may play out differently to our previous experience. We need to look for the gold within, look for the gift.

It is insightful that when that same Church of England report asked for the top qualities young adults look for in a 'perfect church', they spoke highest about inclusion and connection:[141]

- Friendly (79%)

- Non-judgemental

- Passionate

- Social

- Encourages participation

- Listens

- Strong leadership (only 35%)

Identify leaders ahead of time

In leadership it is important to build in order of priority; to watch what God is doing; to anticipate and be willing to invest early; to start simply and then increase what we do as the finance and time resource become possible. We have often applied this principle in our church leadership. For example, we raised funding to appoint young adult leaders at the beginning of our church plant. One year on, we appointed student leaders and three years on, a youth leader. It can be strategic to appoint a leader before the ministry really exists, in order to build it up. In a previous church we watched a whole youth network grow through this principle of identifying (voluntary) youth leaders;

then raising the funds over time to resource them, and setting them out to reach the unchurched through detached youth work.

In order for this to work, the local church must carry a vision to be about reaching the city, not simply resourcing the church they can see in front of them.

Pass me the baton

As in a good relay race, we have to pass the baton. We church leaders have to find ways of passing the baton on to those ahead, but still running alongside at a similar and then decreasing pace for a while longer during the transition period. We have to make space.

The Church locally and nationally must seek to create multiple leadership development pathways. At a local level, we firmly believe that ministers should be actively seeking successors for their own roles, as well as all leadership positions, secure in the knowledge that as they seek Him God will reveal their next assignment because nobody is redundant or retired in His Kingdom. We should always be asking ourselves, 'How can I do myself out of a job?' and identifying, investing into and promoting emerging – often younger – leaders into existing roles, or creating new roles for them. Some ecclesiastical structures can hinder this, but it only takes a little creative thinking to get past them and refocus on the genuine purpose of church: raising disciples who raise disciples.

For every ministry which you are already running locally, are you raising future leaders? Are you seeking to replicate and reproduce this ministry (or another equally good kingdom initiative) further? If you are presently a leader of something within a church, you can already be looking out for how to replicate your experience and gifting into others. Call them an 'assistant leader' or an 'intern', or simply invite them alongside you regularly and begin to share life, wisdom and responsibility with them.

But let us choose pathways that actively raise radical disciples. Discipleship is a buzzword in current Church culture. Leaders have to be careful to assess whether our discipleship culture matches the model of discipleship according to Jesus in the Gospels. Let us not lower the bar. The Christian life is the greatest adventure on earth.

Case Study:

Deeper School of Ministry (www.deeper.training)

Some discipleship and leadership pathways can be more formalised, and lengthy. We do not need to reinvent the wheel, there are various successful models of internships, discipleship years, and short-term mission training in place around the UK already. One year after we planted The Well Sheffield church, we prioritised and financially subsidised the launch of our nine-month discipleship and ministry school, called Deeper. It is designed by people who have led and observed similar schools all over the world, so it integrates and develops personal faith with practical application through immersive experiences in challenging missional contexts.

It is a three-fold mix of prayer/worship, teaching input and radical mission/evangelism, over one to two days per week. It is open to any age, which creates a rich environment both for our youngest (age eighteen) and oldest (age seventy) participants so far. Taught input is only part of the story: it is not a Bible school, it is a school of missionary life. Every week we dig into long sessions of prayer and worship. That is the place of perseverance and revelation where people's characters are truly transformed and breakthroughs come. We go to our local high street each week to share the gospel or prophetic ministry with passers-by. Doing this breaks our own fears, as well as blessing other people. We require participants to be with our city's poor and unpopular people by serving another church's outreach to the Roma community. We teach discipleship, Christian identity and character in the empowerment of the Holy Spirit.

This kind of scheme works well for local churches; it can start small and still be radical. But there is nothing like sending participants away from your context and out of their comfort zone into an alien culture. That is where we have to rely on God's power and strengthening, and we see the gospel in action in new ways. Deeper travels each year to partner with local missionaries around the world: we have travelled to the 'Jungle' in Calais, Nairobi, Helsinki, Philippines, and the Mexican/US border towns. Two generations ago this is what made initiatives like YWAM and Operation Mobilisation so different and effective – it would be a mistake to think that these methods are no longer effective for contemporary young adult development as disciples.

Patterns of church that will help not hinder

There is no perfect local church, but we maintain as others have done that 'the local church is the hope of the world'.[142] Christ's body on earth comes in various shapes and sizes, and local churches seem to deliver brilliantly to certain strengths but significantly miss the mark in some other aspects which are crucial to reaching and keeping young adults in discipleship and mission. The pressing question is how to help existing congregations and individuals get on with discipleship within the present paradigm. What patterns of 'how we do church' need to shift in their design?

Foreign or familiar?

Our present church is part of the Baptist family and most Baptist buildings are more than 100 years old. The careful stewardship of previous generations really blesses us today. But there is a problem if your building's interior still resembles those of the last century! Times have changed. This collaborative, social generation are used to round-table discussions in school and communal workstations. They expect comfortable, stimulating spaces. The layout of a building speaks volumes. Is the environment foreign or familiar to Generations Y and Z? Does it resemble anything from their world of cafés, workplaces, gyms or study hubs? If it does not, then we are sending a clear message: the Church is out of date or inaccessible.

Small, subtle changes, such as the layout of chairs and sofas, signage, a pop-up refreshments station, or quality lighting can make a huge difference. However, the Millennial generation also truly values heritage in buildings and objects: it is part of their appreciation of the 'authentic'. The Well Sheffield's building of 1905 has original wooden pews. We will probably remove them one day, but interestingly it is our young adults who are the most fond of them and the most vocal in wanting to keep them!

Case Study:

KXC Church Plant

KXC, King's Cross Church, was planted in 2010 in central London 'to recklessly give themselves away to God, each other and the people of King's Cross and beyond'.[143] Led by a couple in their thirties, it has grown particularly through young adults, and is representative of a story that is being repeated around the UK by a few churches doing a few things deliberately and well.

Their lead pastors are gifted communicators whose preaching helps to tell the big story of Christianity and to locate young adults within it, helping them to make sense of a complex metropolitan context. They focus on building a strong sense of belonging and community, of addressing local issues of poverty, and the opportunity of raising young leaders.

On Sundays the wooden pews of the rented church they share with a local Ethiopian congregation are packed with young people in their twenties. It is an old former Methodist building in a deprived area of King's Cross London, not the revamped and trendy part of King's Cross which usually attracts Millennials and Generation Z. The older building might not be very practical yet it very obviously houses the presence of God, and that is what is most attractive about it. Their young people love its ambience. They hold multiple services to accommodate their growth.

Unlike the previous Generation X who experimented with church in 'non-churchy' locations like cafés or schools, Generations Y and Z are happy to leave some modern conveniences behind to embrace the heritage feel of old churches. Above all, KXC's emphasis on prioritising and stewarding the presence of God in worship and prayer is the most attractive aspect. Much more than trendy branding, they have brought the life of God to a neighbourhood and a heritage building by creating a contemporary culture which is carefully founded upon the Scriptures.

Analogue theology in a digital society

There is an urgency for our preaching and public presentation to become far more appropriate to the twenty-first century. Many preachers were trained (perhaps thirty years ago) in a modernist methodology of presenting a strong propositional argument via a biblical exposition of a passage. In other words, what some people call 'solid Bible teaching'.

The danger is that we sound like Thomas Gradgrind in the opening of Charles Dickens' *Hard Times* who demanded 'Now, what I want is Facts. Teach these boys and girls nothing but Facts. Facts alone are wanted in life.'[144]

But postmodern young adults are becoming less and less familiar or accepting of the methods and mindsets of modernity. They are raised in a society which rejects metanarrative and is sceptical of the claim of one collection of writings as objective truth – especially if it is 2,000 years old. It questions the motives of any expert public speaker and it longs to know what is really going on underneath the façade. Contemporary young adults in Britain are largely biblically illiterate. Many grow up with zero exposure to the teachings of Jesus, and some imagine He is nothing but a fictional character or a convenient swear word.

Of course, there must always be room for a propositional approach: Jesus is *the* truth, and we are called to proclaim this, using the Bible as our guide. But the tone and medium of communication matters too. In our post-Christian culture, you will be heard much more kindly if you engage with an emotionally engaging and savvy presentation of 'the facts' in a persuasive and collaborative manner.

We live in the midst of a communications revolution: the most popular way Generation Z now learns is by video, not written instructions. If they want to learn a new skill, they will watch it first being performed on YouTube. They love narrative and storytelling – today that is the strongest way to teach. They take inputs from a mix of sources: visual, auditory and kinaesthetic (movement/learn by doing). They hate being 'preached' at if the church minister appears as an expert and they are required to believe something simply because you say it is true. But if you paint an appealing picture and point them in the right direction for good further research (after all, this is the Google generation and they will have their phone in their hand anyway), then you engage their preference for collaboration.

In our teaching and discipleship, we need to allow space for young adults to debate issues and help them to apply the gospel to real life. This means preaching in order to garner an immediate response. These are the experiential generations. We should design our meetings to allow for and to expect an encounter with the truth on the spot, not just mental assent to a set of spoken propositions. As a preacher, this can feel like a loss of control since supplying the 'answers' and application is suddenly out of your hands. But let us remember that Jesus asked 307 questions in the Gospels, and of those 183 questions asked to Him, he only gave a direct answer to three![145]

This is not a matter of anything goes. That is prevalent already in contemporary culture. Do what Jesus did: ask pertinent questions and give people the strong framework of a biblical world view in order to find the right outcome. Presenting options might sound like: 'Jesus said this . . .' or, 'I have found this . . .' Could we recover the New Testament's pattern of communal discipleship, so that our interpretation becomes more of a collaborative, inclusive conversation?

Since podcasts and YouTube are now one of the principle means by which people gather information and assimilate culture, surely it is a no-brainer that Christian mentors and churches must produce more online discipleship content than ever before, to win the ratings war against the louder voices in the vlog-sphere. It is not a case of 'less is more', it is quite the opposite. The young adults you know are always being discipled by somebody or some YouTube channel: so let us engage in the same space and raise our voice too.[146]

The power of an experience

Christians meeting together can be quite an experience. From Sunday services to mid-week fellowship in homes, there is a dynamic, interactive involvement as we gather. People are included, it is never a one-man show. Everyone prays, sings, reads, watches, listens; everyone may partake.

Today's young people are hugely experiential. Theories and facts receive far less value and attention than active experiences. 'Can I interact with it? Can it be touched, smelt, seen?' They love adventure theme parks, shopping in packs, muddy music festivals and substance-induced highs, global travel, visual apps or interactive gaming. This is a 'show and tell' culture. We are now a post-Christian society, which works to the favour of those seeking to 'show and tell' the gospel. It means that young people are very open to new experiences, and when they come into contact with 'church' it is frequently without negative baggage. They are ripe for revival, for a genuine, spiritual encounter with the living God. That is what every church meeting could be like.

It may be surprising to hear that some of the historic practices of the Church, which we take for granted, are very well-attuned and attractive to today's young adults. Engaging in worship is deeply experiential, whether it is expressed by incense, pageantry and mystery, or in a contemporary musical style led by a live band. Cathedral service attendance has grown considerably in the past decade among the young and teen festivals like Soul Survivor and its successors pack in thousands of teenagers, yet their worship sets can be forty-five to sixty minutes long, and the words, the emotions, the depth is never dumbed down. The sacrament of communion is very experiential. Author and pastor Skye Jethani says:

> The Eucharist has another advantage over sermons – it can't be digitised. Communion is an incarnate experience. The bread is held, blessed, broken, given and eaten. Believers gather to pray, confess, absolve and affirm. The entire enterprise requires engagement and activity. It cannot be passively listened to via headphones. The body and blood cannot be downloaded or streamed.[147]

Let us have confidence that when the Church gathers, God's Spirit is present in all His creative, experiential, in-the-moment power.

Author Rachel Held Evans puts this brilliantly:

> The trick isn't to make church cool; it's to keep worship weird . . . You can share food with the hungry at any homeless shelter, but only the church teaches that a shared meal brings us into the very presence of God. What finally brought me back, after years of running away, wasn't lattes or skinny jeans; it was the sacraments. Baptism, confession, Communion, preaching the Word, anointing the sick – you know, those strange rituals and traditions Christians have been practicing for the past 2,000 years. The sacraments are what make the church relevant, no matter the culture or era. They don't need to be repackaged or rebranded; they just need to be practiced, offered and explained in the context of a loving, authentic and inclusive community.[148]

Scratch where people itch

It is imperative that churches publicly address the issues which matter to Generations Y and Z. We should scratch where they itch. What do they care about? What are they afraid of, or just plain confused about?

What are some of the other key issues which Generations Y and Z encounter regularly in everyday life, but are unlikely to be addressed regularly in church sermons?

- Mental health, living with depression, controlling fears and panic attacks
- Relating well to fathers, and God as a loving Father
- Pornography, masturbation, shame
- Relationships: online dating and dating etiquette, marriage, partners

- Exploring sexuality
- The place of contraception and abortion
- The supernatural realm and the occult
- Integrating work and the workplace into the Christian life

For example, when was the last time we addressed publicly (or in personal mentoring) matters of finding a life partner, social action, workplace flourishing, or how to share our faith? A large-scale survey by the UK's Evangelical Alliance found that churches are good at addressing and equipping some areas of life, but poor at others:

> The young adults who took our survey are most likely to say that their church helps them a lot to: connect with God (63%), connect with other Christians (63%), use their skills and gifts to serve God (58%), increase their understanding of the Bible (52%) and transform their life to become more like Christ (50%). Young adults were most likely to say that their church does not really help them: have opportunities to meet a marriage partner (36% said this), in their personal evangelism (27%), to engage in social action (23%), in living out their faith at work (19%) or in developing leadership skills and experience (19%). This indicates that churches need to do more to equip young adults in these areas.[149]

What an opportunity we have to validate a whole-life calling: Christianity worked out in the nitty-gritty of the workplace, parenting, education etc. Never, even subconsciously, saying that church ministry is more 'spiritual' than 'secular' roles. Helping young parents to navigate raising children of faith amid the challenges of social media, Sunday sports, peer pressure, cultural assumptions and so forth.

Help during times of transition

Since a local church is an established Christian community, it can play a really helpful role of building scaffolding around young adults during times when their life patterns mean their social, moral and spiritual foundations are unstable. Research has shown several stages of teen and young adult life when people are most likely to drop away from committed engagement in organised church. They are:

- Youth ages 14, 16, 18 (coinciding with major exam times)[150]
- Students – approx. 75 per cent of teens drop out of church attendance when they move away to university[151]
- Relocation in post-university/early young professional life

We can aid young people to 'stand firm' in their faith (Eph. 6:13-14, NIV) during the inevitable disruption and unpredictable lifestyle of their late teens and early twenties. During these ambiguous transition stages, churches can make simple, clear offers to people that will genuinely help them to remain within Christian community and form them into disciples of Jesus. Making a relational connection is the first step to help a person in their discernment and processing. Miriam Swaffield's academic research into the common factors behind students coming to faith while at university in the UK identifies several key factors which any local church can reproduce with some attention.[152] Of those students who came to faith 100 per cent were first invited and attended church on a Sunday. *Sunday church still works!* Let us make it as easy as possible for young people to access and enjoy it.

The next two most significant factors (91 per cent) were being invited to a small group and 'experienced prayer as powerful and able to change things', followed by a strong welcome and quality preaching. These are the simple things of church that are so important! The four most significant categories for students were: their experience of church; establishing relationships of friendship and mentoring; opportunities; tools to investigate faith for themselves, and encountering the supernatural power of God.

Marketing matters

The aim of discipleship is never to create a church brand or following. Instead we are raising Jesus-like followers. But patterns and style do matter. Nobody needs to be perfect or polished, but we can help ourselves by offering simple, relational and accessible content. The reality is that if the young adult is an existing Christian, they will use a consumer approach to select a new church community. If they are unchurched, they will undoubtedly research you in advance through the internet but your 'stickiness' factor will come because of relationship: will they encounter God's living Spirit, and will they encounter a hospitable welcome?

Ensure that information about the church is accurate, readily available through multiple channels, and appealing to the target audience. Try to understand what people are looking for and help people to make informed choices. For example, good church websites have a section called something like 'what to expect on a Sunday'.

The Sunday experience still matters massively. Are we designing them with the unchurched, or with young people in mind? Do those groups in our city even know or perceive the church as a viable option? We admire the Fusion student network in the UK who have pioneered the #TryChurch hashtag because it presents church as a genuine lifestyle option for young adults to consider.

We have found it is important that when a young person shows some interest, we should be responsive, and not wait very long to be in contact. Responding immediately demonstrates that you value them, plus it is what they are used to in normal life. This is the age of instant communication and feedback. Studies show that young adults remain in congregations who help them to get involved quickly in local church life and in volunteering. It communicates value, that they have something to offer, that you are inclusive and your warm welcome is genuine: even before you know they will have any further connection with you.[153]

138. *The Sunday Times* (London: Times Newspapers Ltd.), 7 April 2019. Author's paraphrase.

139. Remarks of President Donald J. Trump, Inaugural Address, 20 January 2017, Washington, D.C., 'The Inaugural Address', *The White House*, The United States Government, 20 January 2017, www.whitehouse.gov/briefings-statements/the-inaugural-address/ (accessed 5.12.19).

140. Church of England Education Office, *Rooted in the Church: Summary Report November 2016* (London: 2016), p. 3, https://www.churchofengland.org/sites/default/files/2017-10/2016_rooted_in_the_church_summary_report.pdf (accessed 5.12.19).

141. Church of England Education Office, *Rooted in the Church: Summary Report November 2016* (London: 2016), p. 17, https://www.churchofengland.org/sites/default/files/2017-10/2016_rooted_in_the_church_summary_report.pdf (accessed 5.12.19). Bullet points added.

142. Attributed to Bill Hybels.

143. www.kxc.org.uk/story-vision (accessed 5.12.19).

144. Charles Dickens, *Hard Times: For These Times* (London, Bradbury & Evans, 1854), p. 3.

145. Martin B. Copenhaver, *Jesus is the Question: the 307 Questions Jesus Asked and the 3 He Answered* (Nashville, TN: Abingdon Press, 2014).

146. An Evangelical Alliance report found that of committed Christian churchgoing young adults 'Less than half (49%) said that the teaching they find most benefits them is teaching from their church – meaning leaders can't assume that it is their church's teaching that most influences millennials in their congregation. Other forms of teaching which millennials benefit from are podcasts (17%), online blogs (15%), other forms such as books (13%) and social media (4%)'. Evangelical Alliance, *Building Tomorrow's Church Today: The views and experiences of young adults in the UK church* (London: 2015), p. 10.

147. Skye Jethani, 'The Case against Sermon-Centric Sundays', Premier Christianity, 26 September 2019, www.premierchristianity.com/Past-Issues/2019/October-2019/The-case-against-sermon-centric-Sundays (accessed 5.12.19).

148. Rachel Held Evans, 'Want millennials back in the pews? Stop trying to make church "cool"', *The Washington Post*, 30 April 2015, https://www.washingtonpost.com/opinions/jesus-doesnt-tweet/2015/04/30/fb07ef1a-ed01-11e4-8666-a1d756d0218e_story.html (accessed 5.12.19). © 1996-2020 The Washington Post.

149. Evangelical Alliance, *Building Tomorrow's Church Today: The views and experiences of young adults in the UK church* (London: 2015), p. 20.

150. 'In our survey of congregations, parents of young people were asked to say at what age their children started to attend church less often. The average response was 14.5 years old, with peaks of dropping out at age 13, 16 and 18 – ages which broadly correspond to the beginning of secondary school, the end of Key Stage 4 (GCSEs) and the end of Key Stage 5 (A-levels or the equivalent).' Church of England Education Office, *Rooted in the Church: Summary Report November 2016* (London: 2016), p. 5. https://www.churchofengland.org/sites/default/files/2017-10/2016_rooted_in_the_church_summary_report.pdf (accessed 5.12.19).

151. Author's approximation, based on conversations with national Christian student workers

152. Miriam Swaffield, *How are students coming to faith in Jesus at university today? Church Leader's Summary Report* (Loughborough: Fusion, 2018).

153. For indepth research see Matthew Alan James Ward, 'Searching for belonging: an exploration of how recent university graduates seek and find belonging in new church communities' (Durham theses, Durham University, 2016). Available at Durham E-Theses Online: http://etheses.dur.ac.uk/11825/.

CHAPTER EIGHTEEN

A Final Word: What's Next?

It starts with you and me

What's next?

We hope you are stirred and equipped a little more to want to reach and disciple Generations Y and Z. Today's dominant culture presents us with an enormous challenge and at times it feels like it is actively working against this goal. At the same time, we should have great confidence that the message and presence of Jesus is exactly suited to today's young adults, if only somebody would help them to see and experience it. Some of us are hopeful and are engaged with young adults already. Others of us may feel weaker; perhaps our church is one with a 'missing generation'; perhaps our own children are not presently walking with Jesus, or we have watched young people we love making poor decisions.

If you are a Christian reading this, then whoever you are, whatever your situation, age or responsibilities, we all begin from the same place. Before we begin to take a hard look at whether those young adults we know are living as disciples, we must ask ourselves the same question. Before we address how the national and local Church can change, this change needs to begin with each of us. We are first and foremost called as disciples of Jesus. As much as we might be passionate or desperate to see change in the institutions and people around us, it is a guarantee that Jesus' number one priority is radical obedience to His words, ways and wonders in *my* heart and lifestyle.

Jesus said two vital things about this. Firstly, in paraphrase, 'My disciples are those who listen to what I say and put it into action' (Matt. 7:24). Secondly, 'Don't be pointing out the speck of dust in your neighbour's eye and overlooking the plank in your own!' (Matt. 7:3-5).

We find this just as challenging as you do, which is how Jesus intended it. It starts with each one of us taking personal responsibility to live and model the kind of life which those in the emerging generations would wish to imitate. If we are not a radical disciple in the same vein as we see in the pages of the book of Acts, then why should those we are seeking to influence want to be? When we are passionately in love with Jesus, using the ancient spiritual disciplines to train our heart, soul, mind and body towards the worship of God, or at least journeying in that direction, then we are already part of the solution.

Following Jesus is incredibly costly. Thank God that the return on investment is so good! Having the desire to disciple young adults means personally being willing to make the sacrifices and investment necessary to prioritise discipleship. Discipleship often happens at the most inconvenient moments! Think of Jesus' first disciples: some of their biggest breakthroughs came in the middle of the night and at the break of dawn,[154] or after a hot, hungry day crammed with people and problems.[155] We will only have the reserves to reach out to others as we firstly lean-in to deep friendship with God.

We have the extraordinary opportunity to disciple a whole generation. It will require extraordinary commitment. God will provide extraordinary grace. It begins with each of us falling more in love with Jesus, hearing and obeying the words of our Father, in the power of His Holy Spirit.

---

154. Jesus walks on water, Matthew 14:22-33; Jesus appears on the lake shore after His resurrection, John 21:1-14.
155. Feeding the multitudes, Matthew 14:13-21; see also the miraculous catch of fish, Luke 5:1-11.

APPENDIX 1

Tools to help Decision-Making

In our experience, when young adults have a simple framework to apply to a situation it enables them to work through a wise, empowering process before coming to a decision. Mentors can also work through these steps in discussion with individuals and draw them out on each point. A lot about these steps is plain common sense; the extra dimension a Christian mentor can bring is that of theological reflection: how does the Bible and its revelation of God speak into the questions at hand? This can be an especially helpful gift to Generations Y and Z, since they tend to have very low biblical literacy. As the proverb says, 'To answer before listening – that is folly and shame' (Prov. 18:13, NIV).

There follow three simple stages which can help everybody to take wise decisions.

Stage 1: Reflection is the better part of valour (or 'think before you act')

The tried and tested method to think deeply about life, oneself, God, choices or motivations is to use a 'reflective cycle'. This is simply a process that most people go through naturally without being very aware of it when making decisions. But because it is an intuitive thing, there are times when it is very helpful to make these kinds of steps crystal clear.

Models like these are well worth learning off by heart so that people may remember to apply them in all situations, bearing in mind that moving on a stage in each of these cycles can be a matter of moments, or it could take months of time and developments. We are amazed by how often somebody consumed with hurry or worry can miss out a 'stage' of processing a decision, which can mean they deal very poorly with a choice. This would be avoided if they were empowered to use a simple tool like the ones we share below.

Even Jesus did this – He was in a reflective cycle with the Father and Spirit all the time:

> I can do nothing on my own. I judge as God tells me. Therefore, my judgment is just, because I carry out the will of the one who sent me, not my own will.
>
> *(John 5:30)*

A. See It, Do It, Understand It from Causeway Coast Vineyard and Alan Scott.[156] This cycle is designed to propel a person beyond being a spectator in the kingdom life into continual fruitfulness. It may be entered at any point and it is important then to complete each step.

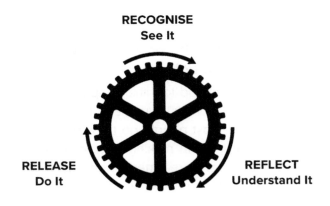

RECOGNISE
See It

RELEASE
Do It

REFLECT
Understand It

B. The Doing Theology Spiral by Laurie Green.[157] This captures the constant interaction between action and reflection. While it was originally designed as a model for forming theology within a group of people, it relates well to today's young adult culture which is so experiential and collaborative.

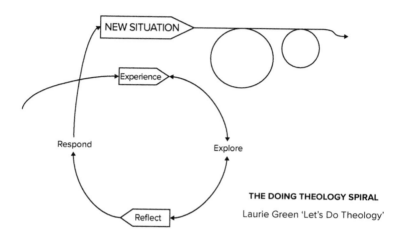

THE DOING THEOLOGY SPIRAL

Laurie Green 'Let's Do Theology'

C. The Learning Circle.[158] This reflective cycle has simple steps that are easy to follow. It helpfully includes the corporate dimension of accountability, which in our experience is often the prompt which a person needs to put their plan into action.

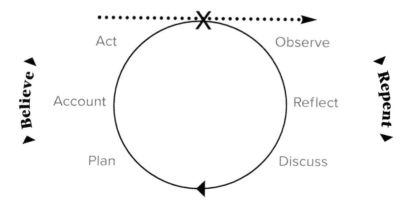

Stage 2: Involve others

> Without wise leadership, a nation falls; there is safety in having many advisers.
>
> *(Prov. 11:14)*

> Fools have no interest in understanding; they only want to air their own opinions.
>
> *(Prov. 18:2)*

In the majority of cases it is helpful for a young adult to widen their circle of input and wisdom so that voices and ideas beyond their own get heard before they make a final choice. In other words: involve other people in your significant decisions. You might be surprised how often people do not do this. A good leader must challenge young people to look beyond the immediate and to stretch themselves in new and uncomfortable ways.

Stage 3: Start somewhere

Finally and simply, try to help young adults to start somewhere. Amid being unable to make major choices, or fear of missing out on others, the kindest and most stable discipleship goal can often be just to start somewhere. To commit for a decent length of time to *something*.

In today's world the options are endless. Skills are transferrable, you can travel on budget airlines, choose your life opportunities. In such a culture the grass may always appear greener elsewhere – I can simply swap contexts, jobs, homes, churches etc.

A lot of what we have done over the past twenty years involves empowering young adults to lead. Empowering them to take ownership for projects and causes, and to run with something significant. At the macro church level we've preached for months on 'Dreaming with God'. We have run training and equipping courses like 'Dreams to Reality' to walk people through steps to take decisions and build-out initiatives. At the micro level, we devote a lot of time to one-to-one chats (usually over a walk in the local park with the dog, or around the kitchen table) with young adults to help them to process their questions, dreams or fears.

But we never leave it there. We always push towards an outcome – an action or a decision drawing upon the principles of the kingdom of God. We help them to ask themselves two vital questions: 'What is God saying?' and 'What are you going to do about it?' and we try to hold them accountable in the time to come as to whether they put that into action.

---

156. Scattered Servants@2018 by Alan Scott. Used by permission of David C Cook. May not be further reproduced. All rights reserved.
157. © Laurie Green, 2009, *Let's Do Theology*, Mowbray, used by permission of Bloomsbury Publishing Plc.
158. Mike Breen, *Choosing to Learn from Life*, (Colorado: Nexgen, 2006), p.55

APPENDIX 2

Discovery Bible Study

A Discovery Bible Study is a discipleship tool which enables people to read the bible together and discover what it has to say to them about God, themselves and others. Simple, memorable questions allow participants to understand the character of God, encourages them to obey what they are learning and help them to share it with others. This interactive model can be used by multiple group sizes: anything from two people meeting over a coffee, a home-group setting or a church gathering. It works well with new believers or seekers, as well as seasoned Christians.

Discovery Passage:

Read the Scripture out loud. Read it again.
Now retell the passage to another person in your own words (this helps us to remember it later)

Discovery Questions:

1. What happens in this passage?

2. What does this passage tell us about God?

3. What does this passage tell us about people?

Obedience

1. How does this change how we see God?

2. How does this passage change how we treat others?

3. How does this passage change how we live?

4. What other questions do you have about this passage?

Multiplication

1. Who can you share this passage and learning with?